Megan,
May all your rockstar dreams come true!

The TransAm Diaries

Stevie D.

Steven "Stevie D." DuPin

Headline Books, Inc.
Terra Alta, WV

Trans Am Diaries

by Steven DuPin

copyright ©2014 Steven DuPin

All rights reserved. No part of this publication may be reproduced or transmitted in any other form or for any means, electronic or mechanical, including photocopy, recording or any information storage system, without written permission from Headline Books, Inc.

To order additional copies of this book or for book publishing information, or to contact the author:

Headline Books, Inc.
P.O. Box 52
Terra Alta, WV 26764
www.headlinebooks.com
800-570-5951

ISBN 13: 978-0-938467-90-8

Library of Congress Number is on file with Library of Congress

PRINTED IN THE UNITED STATES OF AMERICA

Acknowledgments

I would like to dedicate this book to my love, my rock, my best friend, Katie, who challenges me every day to be a better man. As I've said before, you are a sage. You have so much wisdom, yet you always listen patiently to my silly babble. I admire your integrity, your humor, and of course your beauty. ;) You will always be my Princess Bride.

Also, to my pride and joy, Colin and Faith: "When God saw Jesus he sighed, for in Him he saw Himself." Words could never begin to describe the love that fills my heart for you. Thank you for teaching me patience. Faith, even when you refuse to take a bite of something that was your favorite food just the day before. Ohm. You are my best audience. Promise me you will never grow up. My dad, for showing me that a tough guy can also be tender. Even though you were a rolling stone, I always felt loved when I was with you. Thanks for the swagger.

I would also like to dedicate this book to my mama. I know deep down you must've had dreams of your own, but were too humble to ever express them. I hope you found some joy in seeing me go for mine, even though it meant us being apart. Thank you for never discouraging me.

I have so many others to thank— my sisters who have always supported me—Sandy, Donna, and Holly. My wife's lovely family who accepted me even though I may not have fit the mold. Hey, I always knew there was a connection between the Irish and Hillbillies.

Thank you, Cathy Teets at Headline Books, for believing in my story. My publicist, Fred Anderson, who I know I made completely kookoo at times. Remember to breathe, smell the roses, blow out the candle. Jackson and Justin Kelly, Judi "Sketch" Lewinson and Joe Weaver for your artistic graphic talents. You've always had my back on all my projects. Cindy

Broder and Arleen Sorkin, you both have hearts of gold. Bob Broder and David Heisler. My Kentucky family. My surgeon, Dr. Stephen Williams, the "man with the golden hands," thanks for saving my life. The staff at Kaiser Permanente Hospital. All of my friends in the comedy world, many of whom learned to turn hard times into laughs. As Richard Pryor said, the best comedy comes from pain. All of my friends in Kentucky, Florida, Georgia, Los Angeles and wherever your life has taken you. Brian Luttrell for suggesting the title. Elvis, Billy Jack (a.k.a. Tom Laughlin), James Brown, Evel Knievel, Richard Pryor, Abraham Lincoln, Dick Van Dyke. A wide assortment, but hey, I'm a complicated man and no one understands me but my woman. I have stolen from each of you. Thank you for sharing your talents with the world.

There are many more. Those who may have given a nod of encouragement, and even those did not expect much from me, you all have helped fuel my fire. Thanks in advance to the readers who have purchased this book (both of you). I hope you were not disappointed. And best for last, as Colin says: I'd like to thank God for never allowing my light to burn out. I will continue to let it shine.

Prologue

Kentucky has produced some famous literary figures: Wendell Berry, Sue Grafton, Robert Penn Warren, Silas House, Jesse Stuart, Hunter S. Thompson…Larry Flynt. I am not among them. When I was a kid, instead of paying attention in English class, I was busy making my friends laugh. I'd like to think of it as entertaining the troops. I used to think an apostrophe was one of those 12 guys who followed Jesus around. When my teacher made me stay after school to practice cursive, I was excited, because I thought she meant dirty words. I was good at that. I quickly learned that she was trying to get me to improve my penmanship. I wanted to get better, so I practiced writing on bathroom walls and railroad overpasses.

I spent the next 15 years writing my own comedy material, but you don't need to know how to spell "encore" to get one. (It is with an "E," isn't it?) I call my native language Hillbilly Ebonics. I never used to think I would ever try writing a book. I was having too much fun in Hollywood, rockin' the stage and causing mayhem on the Sunset Strip. Then one day, I got the news that I had cancer. Of course, now I had no choice but to write a book. If my life wasn't over literally, I thought it would be over figuratively. Who wants to hang out with someone who's sick and depressed? If I was going to survive, I knew I had to stay busy and maintain a sense of humor, so that's what I did, thanks to some great friends, my wife and my incredible kids.

If it had not been for the people who helped me get through the scariest time of my life, I don't know what I would have done. I believe laughter is the best medicine, so I decided to share some of my crazy stories with others. Hunter S. Thompson may have had "Fear and Loathing in Las Vegas," but I have Fearless and Loitering in Los Angeles.

The following chapters are written how I think and talk. In literature, it's called "stream of consciousness." In Hillbilly Ebonics, the stream is more like a muddy creek. As you read my story, try imagining you and me just kicking back and having a few cold ones (you're buying), while I tell you how I got to where I'm at. (I know, I'm not supposed to end a sentence with a proposition.)

—Stevie D.

1

Walk of Shame

January 4, 2011

It was early morning, another beautiful day in the San Fernando Valley of Los Angeles. Unfortunately, this made the fact that we were on our way to Kaiser Permanente Hospital in Woodland Hills even more unpleasant for me. My wife, Katie, and our 5 month old daughter, Faith, were going with me to get my biopsy and ultrasound. Apparently, I would be sedated through the procedure enough that it could affect my ability to drive. I wasn't sure if a tired, nursing mommy would be more qualified, but we would see. In any case, I guess I expected the weather to reflect my feelings of fear and dread. Why did it have to be so damn sunny?

It had all started one evening in November. Katie's parents were visiting from Lake Arrowhead. We had finished dinner and were joking and having a great time. I was playing with my 2½- year-old son, Colin, when I received a call from a nurse at Kaiser, who informed me that my PSA levels were high from my recent blood work. I had gotten a physical back in March of 2010, but had procrastinated in getting the additional blood work done until recently.

"PSA levels are high?" I ask. "What does that mean?"

She tells me it's regarding my prostate. "Ah-ha! Just as I had suspected," I thought. "I DO have an enlarged prostate!"

She tells me I need to come in for a urine test. I hang up and tell Katie and her parents what the nurse said. I continue to wrestle with Colin (he's winning), not worrying about the news too much. My mother-in-law, Susan Farrell, is a registered nurse. She must've known it could be something a lot more serious, but didn't want to alarm me.

The night before this biopsy, Katie's mom had given me a magazine article about a former NFL player in his 50s who was diagnosed with prostate cancer. It said that younger men were now being diagnosed and encouraged them to get checked. I'd been hearing about how frequently PSA tests are wrong, so of course, a man as young and healthy as I couldn't possibly have this old man's cancer. We all were discussing this fact before I went to bed.

Mrs. Farrell: "Steve, how do you feel? Are you nervous? You will probably be fine. You are so young, you are in great shape...but you never know."

Me: "Yes, I hope those factors help. I keep hearing how wrong these tests often are." (Up until I read this article, I thought at most I may have an enlarged prostate. Now my heart is pounding at the possibility this could be something much worse, and this conversation is not helping).

Mrs. Farrell: "Katie, remember my friend, Helen? Steve, I had this friend who was so healthy. She exercised, only ate organic foods— I mean, chocolate never touched her lips. Well, she was diagnosed with cancer, so you see, you just never know."

Me: "Great. Thanks. I feel so much better now." I force a silly, smile and retire to bed.

After checking in with the nurse in the Urology Department, I begin to observe the other patients in the waiting area. I start feeling very out-of-place because most of the other patients are much, much older than me. Let's get this over with! The nurse calls my name and brings me back. Katie has to entertain the baby, so she stays in the waiting room. After reviewing my records, the nurse tries to comfort my fears with loose conversation: "So I see that your PSA is 4.2. That doesn't necessarily mean anything. I've seen men with much higher scores with no cancer."

"Why is that?" I ask. She can't answer. What the F? I want to get to the bottom of this mystery. Where are Scooby Doo and the Mystery Machine crew when I need them? She tells me the doctor will decide if a biopsy will be necessary. Yay! There is some hope that I will not be violated today!

I'm instructed to remove my pants, but my shirt can stay on. I feel even sillier doing this. Can't they just give me one of those cheap robes where you butt is exposed for easy access?

Hey, Steve, you dropped something. I bend over and—BAM! Promise me you'll call me in the morning, Doc? But, I digress.

The doctor breezes in, and after a brief introduction, he gets right down to business. He asks if there is a history of prostate cancer in my family. I tell him, "No, not that I'm aware of, but my father died of a heart attack at 40." On to the next question. Without blinking an eye, he asks if I smoke. "No," I say, "I have a personal training background. I live a very healthy lifestyle." I was hoping he would say, "Really? Damn, there must be some mistake. What are we doing here? Sorry to waste your time. Have a nice day!" But instead, he gets a little defensive, and raises his voice a notch, "Well, it doesn't mean anything that you are a personal trainer. I'm a doctor, and I know doctors who smoke!"

I say, "I think that's hypocritical. Would someone hire an overweight trainer? I believe in practice what you preach!" Still no reaction, as he stares at his computer, expressionless. This guy would make a great poker player. He finally looks up and says, "We're going in. Turn over and get on all fours!"

I stare at him in disbelief as I ask, "Going in? Going in *where?*"

"I'm going to perform an ultrasound and biopsy." *Whoa! Was it something I said? I don't want to get off to a bad start here, especially before he goes in!*

He turns to pick up something as I roll over. I wish I hadn't peeked, but I couldn't help it. This thing was way too large to enter my body. *Can I get a shot of tequila, please?* He applied some sort of lubricant before he performed the ultrasound (I didn't ask the brand). To say the ultrasound was unpleasant would be a gross understatement. Finally when the "Shawshank" portion of the procedure was complete, he instructed me to lie on my side and pull my knees up to my chest. I'm thinking, *Okay, we got the hard part over with. The biopsy couldn't possibly be more uncomfortable than that!*

I was wrong. I don't know exactly what the procedure entails, except that a very long needle is involved. After rooting around in there for awhile, he warns me that I'm going to hear a pop and feel a zap or sting. He does this seven times! He was right—it felt like he was hitting my prostate with a stun gun. With every jolt, I would flinch and tense every muscle in my body. He tells me to relax and uncurl my toes. *My toes are curled? Can I make that two shots of tequila?*

When the procedure is over, he informs me that he is going to wipe my butt (*what a gentleman*) and to lie back and take some deep breaths before I try to get up. When I feel like I can walk, I am to get dressed and come into his office, along with my wife. As I'm getting dressed, I start to panic. *Meet him in his office? Oh shit, he must've seen a lot of cancer in there! Why does he want me to bring Katie? Is it so she can catch me when I pass out after he tells me I have six months to live?*

I go to get Katie in the waiting area, but she is nursing the baby. Looks like it's just going to be me and the doc. I go into his office to find him busy multitasking, looking over folders, and working on his computer. His erratic energy makes me feel even more unsettled. He barely glances up as he starts to brief me. He begins to explain the formalities, but I can't take the suspense any longer, so I blurt right out, "Did you see anything, Doc?"

He casually replies, "No, I didn't see anything out of the ordinary." *Out of the ordinary? What does that mean? The image of the Virgin Mary on my prostate?* I want to ask for specifics, but he continues by telling me to take it easy for a few days, and that I will receive a call with the results. I ask when to expect it. He said the lab usually takes about five days, so it should be early the following week. He also tells me to expect some blood in my urine for a while. (In my case, a "while" ends up being several weeks.) I'm feeling somewhat relieved as I walk—more like waddle—down the hall to the waiting area. I feel like all the nurses are glancing at me, like they know I've just been violated with a cattle prong. *Hey, at least he said he didn't see anything out of the ordinary. Maybe I'm in the clear?*

Katie and I stop by the pharmacy on the way out of the hospital. As we wait in line, I tell Katie that I don't feel very secure back there. There is numbness and still a lot of lubricant in me. I'm just hoping I don't have an accident. I make up my mind that if this happens, I'll do what any gentleman would do—I'll blame it on our baby.

January 6, 2011

As I drive home in the grueling L.A. traffic, I'm nervously awaiting the call from the urologist who had done the ultrasound and biopsy two days earlier. I'm not going to use his name, let's just call him Dr. Bed-SideManner ("BSM"). This is only Thursday. Why is he calling already? Must be good news! But wait, he left a message about an hour ago. Why wouldn't he just say, "The lab results were negative, have a great weekend!?" He also spoke to Katie, who said he had called our house, but wouldn't give her any info. Hmm…now I'm starting to worry. I think I remember him saying in our very brief post-biopsy meeting that I should hear something early next week; that it usually takes about five days, and if it's negative a nurse would just call and tell me. Wait, the nurse isn't calling--it's him! I don't like this.

The next few minutes seem like an eternity. My heart is racing faster with every second that passes. What if I just don't answer? No, I have to answer. Katie knows he's about to call and I promised her I would call her right after I talk to him. Shit—should I pull over and wait at some remote, tranquil location? Damn—my cell phone rings. How many times should I let it ring? Maybe the news will change if I wait one more? I answer after two rings, and tell myself to sound relaxed.

"Hi, Steve, it's Dr. BSM. Can you talk?" he asks. *Well that depends on what you have to say. I'm stuck in shitty L.A. traffic, about to hear potentially life or death news.* But then again, where is the best place to hear this news? In a very professional, but casual manner, he begins, "So, I got your lab work back and, yes, you do have cancer in 30 percent of the left side of your prostate." Then, speaking to someone else, he says, "Just go ahead a put that folder on the desk." Then, back to me, "So go ahead and drop by my office in the morning, and pick up your information from the nurse." Just as casual as that. I'm thinking, "Sure, I'll just swing by after I pick up a Starbucks, and can I get you a muffin?

"Wait—cancer? Are you sure?" I ask. My head is spinning. I can't process what I'm hearing. This must be a mistake. Cancer! I'm the healthiest person I know! I've exercised for over 20 years! I have a clean diet, and since our son was born two and a half years ago, I rarely drink! *Prostate cancer*? Isn't that an old man's disease?

"Just come by, and the nurse will make an appointment for you," Dr. BSM says. In shock, I say "Should I go to work tomorrow?" In a condescending tone, Dr. BSM replies, "Of course, you were planning to go to work, weren't you?" *No, I was just looking for an excuse to get out of it, and this seems like a good one.* "Yes," I answer, but before I can elaborate, Dr. BSM interjects, "So go to work." (He is interrupted again as he speaks to a nurse about something unrelated to my case. "Did he call you back? Can you leave him a message?") *Damn, doctor, can we focus here?* I'm tempted to hang up on him.

Finally getting back to me, Dr. BSM continues, "So, after you pick up your folder, we're going to discuss your options: radical surgery, chemo, pellets. I'm going to recommend a radical prostatectomy because of your young age. "Oh, by the way, I'm leaving town tomorrow. I'll be gone for three weeks. I'll see you when I return. *Ok, bye now. Got to reserve a tee time!*" (Ok, I made that last part up, but it's how I felt.)

I didn't want to hang up. I had a million more questions, but I thanked the doctor and that was it— I had cancer! Not only did I have cancer, but I also had the next three weeks to walk around with it dazed and confused. It was a cool winter evening and the sun was setting in the San Fernando Valley, but suddenly I was burning up. I rolled down my windows, and tried to wrap my head around the news that this doctor had just casually given me. What's the worst case scenario? Hair loss? I've always used my hair as a crutch in my comedy act. On stage, I joke that I've had the same "Keith Partridge" haircut since I was in the 8th grade. This may be a chance for me to step out of my comfort zone and mix it up with new material! I promised Katie that I would call her back, but I'm only 10 minutes from home. Usually when I'm very close, I call Katie and she opens the door so Colin can stand at the door wait for me. When I'm walking down the sidewalk, I can always hear him, "Da, Da, Da Da…home!" It's the best part of my day. I decide not to call. I'll wait and tell her when I get there.

My head is spinning. I'm still perspiring, and I'm not thinking clearly, so I need a few minutes to try to figure out a way to break the news. Since I didn't call her back, Colin isn't waiting for me at the door. I rush in and try to get to the bathroom before I have to face her and our babies. (I have to use the restroom a lot these days, which led me to have this prostate business checked in the first place.) Katie is sitting on the couch with Faith, and immediately asks if I spoke to the doctor. I answer "Yes" very quickly, trying to keep moving. "Yes, uh, we'll talk about it in just a minute."

She doesn't let me off the hook that easily, and asks, "What did he say?" I see a look of fear and sadness in her eyes. I keep moving and answer, "I'll tell you in just a minute." While I'm in the restroom, I try to think of a good way to tell her. There is no good way to tell your wife and mother of your two small children that you have cancer.

I emerge from the bathroom and find her staring at me and waiting. I walk closer to her and whisper, not wanting Colin to hear. "I have it. Let's please try to keep it together for the babies. I don't want them to see us cry." Katie immediately starts asking questions—"How much cancer is there? How long do I have? What will we do?" I can't answer any of them. She calls her parents and tells her mom first. I didn't tell anyone the first night, I just wanted to try and let it all sink in. Neither of us really has any idea what prostate cancer is, or what its treatment entails.

Katie was extremely brave that night. When we went to bed, she expressed her fears about how we would take care of the family. Katie has been a stay-at-home mom since our son was born. Would she need to go back to work, and where? Am I going to be out for months, or will I recover at all? Since I had just learned of this cancer in a three-minute conversation that evening, I had no answers for her. Tears fill my eyes and I tell her I'm sorry. She had taken a huge chance on marrying me for other reasons: I was in the unpredictable entertainment industry, and lived a very selfish life before she came along. But she believed in me! I was afraid to fall asleep because I was afraid I would have dreams of dying. Eventually, I was able to fall asleep. Luckily, I didn't dream of my demise

I think everyone is curious about how they would handle this type of news. You've seen dozens of TV shows and movies about brave people battling cancer. Could I be so brave? The thought of being in this situation is so frightening that of most of us just choose not to dwell on it. I remember the story of the courageous college professor, Dr. Randy Pausch, and his touching speech, which I saw on YouTube. It's amazing how this guy was still so positive and upbeat, battling his disease. In his speech, he said he likes to have fun; that he doesn't know how NOT to have fun. I feel the same way. I am generally an upbeat, very active guy. However, this type of news could really take the wind out of my sails. When people ask me how I stay so positive all the time, I jokingly say, 'Ignorance is bliss!' Now that I know I have cancer, would it make me lose my naiveté? Would I become a bitter, self-loathing, asshole?

The morning after receiving the news, I had a couple of people to train. Although I have been a professional comedian for years, I maintained my personal training business, so I wasn't able to "drop by" the doctor's off right away—I had to wait until I was finished at around noon. When I arrived at the Kaiser urology department, I stood in a long line until my name came up.

At first they couldn't find my file. The receptionist and another nurse looked around. The receptionist was saying, in a loud voice, "It should be here. Dr. BSM said he would leave it." Looking more, I hear, "The patient's name is Dupin, and it is prostate cancer." I feel completely embarrassed, and I'm not sure why. Is it because of the cancer, or because it has something to do with *that* area of the body? I have to remind myself, "Hello! Everyone is here in the urology department because they have a problem in *that* area!"

They can't find the file. A-ha, I knew this must be a mistake! I bet the lab called Dr. BSM right after we hung last night and told him there was a mistake; that my file had gotten switched with that of an old man! Dr. BSM would've called me back, but he was busy making his tee time! Shit! They find my folder. It's yellow with a large white sticker on the front that says "Steven Dupin—PROSTATE CANCER."

The nurse tells me my appointment with the urologist will be in three weeks. Three weeks???!!! That's way too long! Will I even be alive then? I need an earlier appointment! "P l e a s e put me on the cancellation list," I say to one of the nurses. "I'll sit right here in the lobby and wait!" OK, the nurse agrees to put me on the cancellation list, but still says, "See you in three weeks!"

Thoughts are running through my mind as I'm driving home. *How long have I had this? HOW LONG DO I HAVE?* As I'm leaving the Urology Department, I turn the folder over, to hide the big white sticker, **PROSTATE CANCER.** At every red light on the way home, I'm tempted to peek inside the folder. I'm afraid I will open it and see, in big, bold letters, **"HEY, CANCER PATIENT, SORRY ABOUT THE NEWS! HOPE YOU HAD A GOOD LIFE!"**

I rush in the door and briefly look inside the folder. There are some lab sheets with numbers on them, a brochure with a number for a counselor and support group, and a brochure with an old man on the front that reads, *Prostate Cancer and Your Treatment Options.*

Katie and I look over the lab results together, and start to get even more frustrated. I have no idea what any of this stuff means. I throw the folder on the table and immediately decide to call my previous doctor to request my records. I had my prostate checked a couple of years before. Would anything from that appointment or be helpful? I call Kaiser and ask if my old records had been transferred. They check the computer and find that they were not. I'm not even sure what it would mean if they were, but I was trying to figure out how long I could have possibly had this. Had it spread? Is it in my bloodstream or my brain? Damn, I start to get paranoid. I had noticed that my scalp seemed to be tender on one side when I shower. *Yep, must be cancer in my brain!* I'd also been losing weight the past couple of years. I kept chalking it up to stress of new babies, working more, taking in fewer calories.

I decided to take a brochure out of the PROSTATE CANCER folder and go into the other room and read it over, alone. As I opened the brochure, the first thing I saw was a section titled *Life Expectancy*. Ok, now here's the info I needed! It read, "Average life expectancy for prostate cancer: five years." Five years ? No, I need 45 years! What the F? As I'm about to pass out, I review more, and it states that the average age for prostate cancer is 72. That is a cruel damn joke! I vow not to read more until I can be assured it's from another source besides a geriatric brochure.

Now, about this prostate exam that I had two years earlier, when I was with another insurance company– I had noticed I had been getting up and peeing two or three times a night. Having some knowledge of fitness, I just felt like something was funky in my body. I had also been losing weight. I chalked it up to all the factors previously mentioned, but deep down I felt like something just wasn't right. Years prior, when I would be in the gym, I would see those commercials for old men needing to control their frequent trips to the bathroom with medication for their enlarged prostate. Hmm...I seemed too young for this, but I wanted to go get checked out. My theory was that I spend hours every day stuck in L.A. traffic, and had done some damage to my prostate as a result of repressing my urinating urges!

When my son was just a few months old, I had decided to have a check-up and make sure I was healthy. I didn't have health insurance for the first 12 years that I lived in Los Angeles. It was Katie who strongly encouraged me to be more responsible and get covered. In the past I had only gone to the doctor in emergency situations—broken bones, dental infections, etc. I was referred to a doctor in Tarzana, had seen him a couple of times and thought he was very pleasant and personable. I went in for this particular appointment because of my prostate concerns, and he remembered that I had a baby, and asked about him. Impressive! I was obviously nervous about having a man violate the forbidden zone, which is what they do with a prostate exam. I was never sure how to pronounce his last name, so I asked and he casually replied, "Just call me Sam." *Just call you Sam?* I was thinking, *No, let's keep this very, very professional!* I was then instructed to drop my pants, bend over and hold onto the table. *Damn, this is not the time to remember the scene from Chevy Chase's movie "Fletch"! ("Ever serve time, Doc?")*

I tell myself to just bite the bullet! Luckily, I didn't feel his other hand or both hands on my shoulders (as the old joke goes)! After the manual exam, he told me my prostate was fine, and that I was probably just drinking a lot of water before bedtime. I think I would know if I was downing a liter or of water right before I went to sleep, but whatever, I really want to trust him on this one. *Thanks for, uh, checking, anyway!* Awkward! For reasons unknown, he didn't think it would be necessary to do the additional blood tests to check for prostate cancer. I'm pretty sure I had it then, two years before it was diagnosed by Dr. BSM.

I got a call from Dr. BSM, sounding busy and preoccupied as usual. "Hi, Mr. Dupin? It's Dr. BSM. I have an email from my nurse asking if I received your records from your previous doctor. I never received your records. I don't know what she's talking about." I was just glad to have him on the line, because I wanted to get some info ASAP. I still felt in the dark about the condition. "Anyway," he continued, "I never received those records. Is that all?"

"Well, Doctor," I explained, "I'm just trying to figure out how long I've had this. Could I have had it two years ago? How much time do I have? I have two small children here and a wife. I need to be around a long time." Dr. BSM briskly replied, "Did you look at the folder? All of your lab results are in there— your T-level, your Gleason score." I think, *My what and my what?* I have no idea what this could possibly mean. All I remember from the paperwork was a lot of numbers that I couldn't interpret. Dr.

BSM says, "I see you have an appointment with me on the 26th. We'll discuss everything then. You're going to be fine, after we remove the prostate."

"Remove?" I say, " Isn't that thing important? Who will remove it? Who will perform the surgery?"

"I will!" says Dr. BSM. As he tries to hang up, I bombard him with more questions. This guy is busier than the Tasmanian Devil. I'm definitely not feeling comfortable with the thought of him removing and an organ so delicate and important as the prostate! The prostate is responsible for my ability to pee pee and, more importantly, get erections! He hurries to get me off the phone with a quick, "I'll see you on the 26th. In the meantime, read the over the information in the folder."

After I hang up, Katie and I start hustling for information. We both grab our laptops and simultaneously Google the two words I will be hearing a lot: PROSTATE CANCER!

2

Little Drummer Boy

I was born in Owensboro, Kentucky, a small, working-class town with a population of around 45,000. That was the population when I was growing up there, and I believe it's still the same population today. Some people get out, while others stay and reproduce, so the population stays even. I read a few years ago that there are more fast food restaurants per capita in Owensboro than any other city in the U.S. I don't remember many fast foods joints when I was growing up, but then again, we rarely ate out. There were two factors preventing us from enjoying the white trash pleasures in life like surf and turf at Sizzler—no money, and no car.

Owensboro is also the hometown of Johnny Depp. That's not something that mattered when I was growing up, since I moved away before his *21 Jump Street* debut. I remember visiting Owensboro about ten years ago, and reading an article in on the front page of the newspaper: *Johnny Depp Sends Grandmother Depp Roses*. That was big news in the small town. I once sent my grandmother a male stripper as a joke. It didn't make the newspaper.

Times were lean with my single mom supporting her four children—three girls and myself—on very minimal wages from the factory where she worked. (She recently retired after 44 years, still on the assembly line, making below what is minimum wage in California.) My mom made many sacrifices, for which I'm forever grateful. Along with her shitty factory job, she would also sometimes waitress at the Moose Lodge to try to make ends meet. I remember standing at the bus stop one cold winter morning, along with another neighbor kid, whose mother also worked there. He remarked that the guys at the

Moose Lodge would get drunk on the weekends and grab our moms' butts. I was stunned, and sickened. I was too young and naive to ever have even thought of that. I wish he hadn't either, because I never forgot it. My mom was a very attractive lady. I'm sure she had many opportunities to date, but she never did. We were so poor, I recall occasions when my mom would heat a can of soup for us kids to share, and claimed not to be hungry, so there would be more for us. My mom would've made the perfect housewife, but unfortunately, she made very bad choices in men. And with those choices also went her self-esteem.

Growing up in a house full of girls, I was never good at sports, but I could do a mean French braid! (A little sexist I know, but that joke has gotten a lot of mileage in my stand-up act.) My mom had my older sisters, Sandy and Donna, from her first marriage. I was from her second marriage, and my younger sister, Holly, was from her very brief, third marriage. I always used to say it was up to me to be the man of the house, but the only problem was we already had a man—my sister Donna. Donna was like a butch Marsha Brady, with long blond hair and muscles! She would wear flannel shirts with Sears Toughskins jeans (the hard denim with the built-in patches on the knees). She would bust into my room and with some bass in her voice announce, "Mama said git up, breakfast is ready! But first we gonna wrestle!" She would then proceed to get me in a headlock and body-slam me around my room. I later discovered that a hot blow dryer makes a great weapon. I was, and still am, a master of the art of blow drying.

Sandy and Donna were later forced to move in with their dad for their own safety, after Holly's father made attempts to break into our house, after the divorce.

I was a lonely kid, spending my days playing in solitude with my Hot Wheels and G.I. Joes, or riding my bike. My bike was my pride and joy. If you've seen the movie *Citizen Kane*, my bike was my Rosebud. I had a paper route, which allowed me to earn money to buy parts for this bike. I built that bike one part at a time with my bare hands. One day I came home and my Rosebud was gone. Some damn hoodlums had taken my prized possession! I never did find out who did it. But when I do, I still owe them a kick in the nuts.

Father Greg Boyle (who happens to be my wife's cousin) writes in his book, *Tattoos on the Heart,* there is a hole in almost every gang member's heart in the shape of this father. That was certainly how it was, for me.

I missed my dad every single day. He and my mom divorced when I was 4, and he went to live in Louisville, about two hours away from Owensboro. I wanted to go camping, ride motorcycles and play catch with him. To this day I have an unhealthy resentment toward the game of baseball, because it's synonymous with dads and their sons.

Since we didn't have a car or a telephone during my early years, my grandfather (Pa-Paw) would usually come by on Saturday mornings to take us to the grocery store to stock up for the week. We ate a LOT of bologna! My mom would get creative with it. We would get fried bologna for breakfast instead of the more expensive bacon, and cold or fried bologna sandwiches for lunch with mayo on white bread. (White trash cooking tip #1: Cut four slits in the sides of a slice of bologna when frying, to keep it from curling up. Tip #2: Along with everything else, only fry in bacon grease, which is usually found in a Folger's coffee can on the stove.) When I was around 13 years old I was eating a bologna sandwich for lunch one day. I was about halfway finished, when I stopped, took a long look at the bologna and thought to myself, "What the hell is in this stuff? What part of a cow or pig is bologna? This is poor people food, and it's poison." I threw the sandwich in the trash and vowed to NEVER eat bologna again. I still don't eat bologna or any mystery meat. Besides, I hear that stuff can give you cancer.

Usually toward the middle of the week we'd run out of some item, so I was forced to make trips on my bike to the grocery store. Now the problem with this was that we were also on food stamps. Kids are very impressionable, and I was embarrassed to use food stamps. With food stamps you can only buy the basic essentials—no candy—so I couldn't even get a little Snickers bar for my troubles. I would run in and grab what I was supposed to get, but then I would case out the checkout line and wait until the coast was clear. I didn't want anyone that I knew to see me using food stamps. Sometimes I would find Coke bottles and return them to the grocery store, where they would give me 5 cents for the little ones, and 10 cents for the 32 oz. size. I would always try to keep a little cash in my pocket for emergencies. That way if I was ever in the checkout line and a cute girl from my school came up behind me, I could hide my food stamps, pull out my cash and use my hillbilly charm on her: "Hey, aren't you in Mrs. Trunnel's class? Can I buy you something? How 'bout some bologna?" I imagined her saying, "No, but I'll take a Snickers!" I was also afraid the cashier would bust me with, "Hey Stevie, why aren't you using your food stamps today?"

One of the cashiers at the grocery store was the mother of NASCAR driver Darrell Waltrip and future driver Michael Waltrip. (Darrell is the voice of "Darrell Cartrip," the race announcer in the Disney movie *Cars.*) Now, I wasn't a NASCAR fan, but I was a fan of fame! I watched variety shows and listened to the radio and records, and they all represented to me a way out. I would always go to Ms. Waltrip's checkout line, just to talk to someone who was related to somebody famous. Maybe I thought it was contagious? Also, around this time I had a friend with whom I went to elementary school, Mark Higgs. He had an older brother, Kenny, who played for the University of Kentucky Wildcats. Kenny was in the paper and on television a lot. One day when I was over at Mark's house playing in the yard, he mentioned that his brother was home visiting. "Can I see him?" I asked. I knew nothing about basketball; I just knew he was famous in Kentucky, and I had never actually met anyone who had been on this magical box called television. "Yeah, man," Mark said. "Let's go in."

I followed Mark down the hallway of their small house. (Every house in our area was the same shape and size—very small, and square.) I immediately could hear some of the coolest, funkiest music I'd ever heard to pumping from the back room. We got closer, Mark knocked and went in. I heard him say, "Hey, my friend Stevie wants to meet you." I stepped in and saw Kenny on his bed looking at magazines. He looked very chill.

Kenny said, "What's up, little man?" or some cool shit like that. I was too nervous to remember. I didn't ask for his autograph or have anything to contribute to the conversation like, "How do the Cats look this year?" or "Good game last week!" I was just excited to see someone who had gotten out! I think I said, "Nice to meet you," or something, and Mark and I turned and walked out! It was a very quick exchange, but made a lasting impression on me, nonetheless. *"Damn,"* I thought, *"Too bad I don't know how to play basketball! I wonder if there's a French Braid World Series?"* By the way, my buddy Mark went on to play for the Miami Dolphins as a running back, and he is only 5'7." Anything is possible!

I went to Foust Middle School for the 6th and 8th grades. It was located in the older, sketchier part of town. Lower income public school students went there. It was next to the housing projects, railroad tracks and other depressing landmarks. I just wanted to keep my head down, and lay low until I could figure out a way to get the hell out of this town. Did I mention that I was also very small and thin? I believe the same way that overweight people emotionally overeat, I emotionally under-ate. I was always nervous and insecure. I'd look around and think, *"I need muscles to survive around here."* But that wouldn't happen for a long time. I sucked so badly at sports that once in the 6th grade, our P.E. class had just ended and we were about to go to lunch, but our teacher had what he thought was a humorous idea. He made me and a very overweight female student have a free-throw shooting contest. Now I'm not talking about a game of 21. No, the rule was the class couldn't go to lunch until one of us made a free-throw. After several air balls and countless minutes, I switched my tactic and began shooting granny-style (between my legs). I thought, "The hell with trying to pretend I know how to play this game! If I don't sink one soon, I'm going to get a serious beat-down after school!" The girl ended up making a basket first.

Obviously sports were not my forte, but I thought I would give it another try. When I was in the 7th grade we had moved across town into some new government apartments, so I had to switch schools. I desperately wanted to fit in, so I signed up for football. Not only had I never played football, but no one had ever so much as explained the game to me. It was pathetic, but somehow I stuck the season out. I remember being in the locker room at the end of a training week, and the coach would announce the starting lineup for the upcoming game. I always prayed my name would be called, but it never was. I dreamed of intercepting a pass and running it back to score a touchdown! While the crowd cheered, the coaches would look at each other and say, "Where the fuck has this kid been? He's amazing!" However, unlike the movie *Rudy*, I never even got to touch the football in a game that season. The closet I ever came was when I was put in a game for 45 seconds for a punt after we had a dominating lead. That was the end of my football career.

Reading was not a requirement, or even encouraged in my house growing up. My wife is still surprised when we're reading a classic children's book to our kiddos, and I tell her I've never read it or even seen the movie. *Bambi, Dumbo, Snow White*…the list goes on and on. However, I CAN tell you about anything you want to know about *The Jeffersons* or a *Good Times* episode!

The one thing that did interest this non-athletic, non-book-reading little heathen was music, and more specifically, the DRUMS! However, it took money to own one of those magical-looking drums kits. The only way I was ever going to learn to play the drums, and beat out my frustrations to rhythm, was to join the school band. Now I know what you're thinking: the marching band is *not* the best way to earn street cred, and could actually encourage beat-downs. I later understood this scientific fact and hung up my marching boots before entering high school. No one over the age of 12, besides Michael Jackson, has ever looked cool wearing a Sgt. Pepper jacket!

The only parade I actually marched in, I was required to play the enormous bass drum. There is a chain of command in the drum line, starting with crash cymbals, and then bass drum, before you graduate to the coveted snare. The snare and timbales are the only cool percussion instruments in a marching band. Wait, is that an oxymoron? "Cool instrument" and "marching band?"

I was a newbie in the band when the Thanksgiving Day parade arrived, and our usual bass drum player was sick and unable to march. Usually the bass drum players are on the husky side. Today, I believe the politically correct term would be "calorically challenged." In a panic, our band director instructed me that I would be carrying and playing the bass while, of course, also marching. I probably weighed 90 pounds soaking wet, at 12 years old, so I looked like I was carrying a Volkswagen. To the spectators it looked like the bass drum had legs. After about three blocks, my knees began to buckle and I started to lose the beat. Somehow I made it to the end of the parade and was immediately demoted back down to cymbals.

I joined the marching band along with my best friend since the first grade, Kenny Riley. Our band director's name was Mr. O'Hara. Mr. O'Hara must've been 89 years old. He was the same band director who was there when my sisters, aunts, uncles and mom went to this school, and he always looked 89 years old! Kenny and I eventually worked our way up to snare drums, where we would stand side-by-side in the back of the room, to Mr. O'Hara's right. Now, Kenny and I would always joke around. On one particular song, *Soul Rock*, Kenny and I had a dance routine down where we would perfectly choreograph our spins, which would always infuriate Mr. O'Hara. Being in a middle school marching band is no joking matter. Conducting his delinquent orchestra in front of the chalk board, Mr. O'Hara would load up a couple of erasers with tons of chalk dust and have them on his music stand, ready to fire. When Kenny and I would act up, he would launch them at lightning speed! Now I don't recall ever receiving a direct hit, but Kenny would always get nailed! Kenny had a large Afro and the erasers would hit him in the head, leaving a huge cloud of chalk dust and a dent in his hair. Mr. O'Hara, I'm sorry for all the aggravation we caused you. I wish I had your address; I'd like to send you a card for your 90th birthday!

Kenny and me, top-right. Looks like he has still has chalk in his hair!

3

Wayward Son

My mama (Southern slang for "mother") was born in Calhoun, Kentucky, a very small town about 25 miles from Owensboro, population 12. (Actually, I made the population up, but I'm only off by a couple thousand). I remember my mamaw (grandmother) telling me of how she met my papaw and how he "courted" her. She told me her family, the Vanovers, and his family, the Denos, lived down the road from each other. Papaw would go to her house and they would sit on the front porch swing or go for walks (she may have conveniently left out a few stories involving moonshine). Anyway, my grandmother had a brother who would do the same thing with Papaw's sister. After a brief courtship of swingin' and walkin', both couples ended up getting married. Now this means my mom has double cousins. Not quite in-breeding, but white trash enough to give me a headache when I try to do the math.

My grandparents were very poor. My grandfather, Alonzo Deno, had to drop out of school in the 3rd grade to help his father work on the farm. He never learned to read or write. Apparently, the Kentucky country school curriculum was way behind back then. Either that or maybe he just never attended much school before the 3rd grade. He still worked on a farm when my mother was a little girl. The Deno family actually lived on someone else's farm, where my grandfather worked the fields, pulling a plow behind a mule from sunup to sundown. There must be an easier way to make a buck.

The meals consisted almost entirely of what was grown or raised on the farm. Dora, my mamaw, would tell me how she would go out in the yard, grab a chicken by its neck, swing it around to break it, and then prepare it for dinner. If people had to do this now, there would be a lot more vegetarians. My papaw used to love see me get grossed out when he would sometimes make himself a scrambled egg and cow brain sandwich for breakfast. He loved it! My mama tells me stories about how they would go into town on Saturdays for their basic needs— sugar, flour, etc.—and how she was sometimes allowed to get a piece of candy. She's also told me of how they didn't have any electricity; just one coal-burning oven. I always would picture my mama as Laura Ingalls from *Little House on the Prairie*:

"Ma, can I get just one piece of candy? I've been real good, honest I have."

"Ok, Half Pint, but just one."

When my mom was a teenager, the family moved into town so my grandfather could get a better gig with more security. He got a job with the Owensboro Municipal Utilities street department, where he worked for 38 years. There were times when the family did not have a car, so my grandfather would walk all the way across town, many miles, and still be the first to arrive. No wonder I still can't sleep past 5:00 a.m.! Must be in my genes.

My grandfather was diagnosed with lung cancer when he was 60 years old. He was a lifelong smoker, who had rarely, if ever been to the doctor. By the time they caught it, it was too late. My grandfather had never taken a sick day in his 38 years with OMU, but now had no choice. It was very sad to see this strong, proud man withering away. Just a month or two before he passed away, he asked me if I had an extra bike he could borrow. I had a paper route at the time and had two bikes I used— Schwinn "heavy duties," as they were called. They look just like a beach cruiser, without gears. One was in a lot worse shape than the other, so I gave him that one. The day I gave it to him, he challenged me to a race to the end of the street. Now, I was an avid BMX rider. I rode my bikes every second of the day that I could. I had no video games, and obviously no reading requirements, so I'd ride—building ramps over trash cans in the street, and any other stunts I could concoct (no helmets or pads, of course). He kept teasing me about how he could beat me. I'd never even seen my grandfather ride a bike, and I was aware he was very sick, so I did not want to beat this weak old man in a race. I finally gave in and said, "Ok, Papaw, let's do it!" When we started out I was just going to pretend to be trying, but stay close enough to make it look like I was going for it. We counted it down and took off. It was pretty even for about the first 20 yards and then he started to pull ahead. I kicked it up a notch, but he was still ahead, and three-quarters of the way down the street, I was really pumping, but he was still winning and laughing. *What the… How is it possible that this old man is beating me?* He won the race and continued laughing! I'll never forget that day.

My mom was a raven-haired beauty in high school. I have her class picture from her last year of high school, the 11th grade. Her beautiful black hair is cascading over a borrowed faux mink shawl. She looked like Ava Gardner. I find it amusing the stamp on the bottom of her picture says "Hollywood Studios." My mom married her high school sweetheart, a handsome blond guy named Don. Beautiful couple. Too bad it didn't last long. They divorced when my sister Donna was 3 years old. I won't go into every one of her marriages; I'll just say she has made very bad choices in men, especially her current husband, whom she has been with off and on, but mostly on, for over 30 years. He is the epitome of a redneck. No, I take that back—even some rednecks may have one or two redeeming qualities. I have yet to find one in him. He is an angry, insecure, evil little man. A racist, a bigot and a wife beater, who mocks everything he doesn't understand, which is just about everything. Way to pick 'em, Mom! You deserved so much better. I won't give him a name credit for this book. Let's just call him "Shit for Brains" (SFB)—another Uncle Ricky catch phrase.

Mom and SFB married when I was 13 and his true colors came out almost immediately. (SFB also had three kids from previous marriages whom he expected my mom to raise.) I witnessed SFB give my mom her first beating when I was in the 9th grade. My sister Donna was moving to Michigan, so my mom and her brother Melvin met her out at a lounge for a goodbye drink. SFB was on the road, (he's a truck driver).

When he returned, he was so infuriated, he beat her. I saw him punch her, throw her against the wall and kick her, before she managed to break away, running out of the house, screaming for someone to call the police! I was pulling at him, but because of my size, there wasn't a lot I could do, so I followed them outside, picked up the garden hose and started spraying him with water! Desperate times call for desperate measures. The police arrived shortly thereafter, but my mom was so scared, she and SFB laughed and told them it was just a silly argument. *Great! This is going to be an interesting living situation!* This scenario repeated itself several times. There is nothing more embarrassing than to have your neighbors standing outside gawking, while the police mediate your family's white-trash drama. The amazing thing is the police never arrested SFB. I remember watching the O.J. Simpson trial, and hearing about similar incidents where the police arrived after being called by his wife, Nicole Brown-Simpson, and never made an arrest. At least the star-struck LAPD officers probably got an autographed football for their troubles. I'm not an expert, but I assume SFB was never arrested because my mom wouldn't press charges. You can't help someone who's not willing to help herself. We all know how it turned out for Nicole. I only pray the same thing doesn't happen to Mama.

After another blow-up with SFB, I left and rode my bike across town to my dad's apartment and informed him that I was moving in with him. (He had only moved from Louisville a couple of years earlier). He told me that his apartment was too small and I would need to wait until he got his settlement from his accident. The settlement would allow him to get a house. "No can do," I said. "I am not going back there, period!"

My dad must've seen I was serious, so he gave in and said, "Ok, let's go get your stuff." My dad drove me in his truck, and when we pulled up outside my mom's house, he reached behind his seat and pulled out the fat end of a pool stick. Uh-oh, I didn't want my dad to get arrested, but I wasn't going to be too sad when dad cracked SFB's head. My dad told me to go in and get my stuff! Luckily for SFB, he hadn't laid a hand on me at this point (the coward waited until after my dad passed away for that), but he must've seen my dad pull up, because he was already on the phone calling the cops when I walked in. What a little bitch! I mocked him saying something like, "Calling the cops to save you, tough guy?" After grabbing a few things, I ran back out as fast as I could, and jumped in my dad's truck. I guess my dad had enough common sense not to come in and make matters worse, unless it was necessary. As we drove off, my dad said we were going to the police department to speak to a juvenile officer about custody. *Good plan,* I thought. We arrived and were instructed where to go. After meeting with a juvenile officer, he took us into his office, where my mom and SFB arrived minutes later. The officer began to ask questions about what was going on. I immediately chimed in that this man was abusive to my mom and everyone else in the house, and I had witnessed him beating my mother! Not only was I leaving, I wanted this motherfucker to be arrested!

The officer turned to my mother and asked her point blank, "Is this true?"

I stared at Mom thinking, *Ok, here's your chance to be saved!* I will never forget how she looked directly at the officer and said, "No." *What?* I couldn't believe my ears! How could she defend this man? The officer then started into some rhetoric about how this sounds like another case of an insubordination, teenagers need discipline, blah, blah. I just stared in disbelief.

Mama and me- Easter duds.

I moved in with my father in October of 1981, and he died less than three months later. Unfortunately, my mom is still with SFB and nothing has changed. Weakness is not a virtue. I love my mama very much, but I would rather die on my feet than live on my knees.

4

Panic, Prayer, and Research

Within 24 hours of receiving the cancer news, Katie was on it, like an all-points bulletin. While she was working the phones, the Internet, and scrambling to get information, I had other thoughts running through my mind. As I was sitting in morning traffic, looking around at all the other commuters going about their normal, daily routines, I started feeling so sorry myself. I've busted my ass hustling out here for over 20 years, and been rejected a thousand times, but I've always gotten back up. I've appeared on television, worked my way up through the comedy ranks, and now things are starting to happen for me as a producer. I've been incredibly blessed with a beautiful, caring wife, and two healthy children who have totally stolen my heart. Sorry, Cancer, but there's no way I'm going out like this! Just then a script idea came to mind:

Outline

A man has been living a selfish, egotistical life of womanizing and partying. He has a good heart deep down inside, but has made many sacrifices in pursuit if his dreams. He meets a girl who throws a kink in his plan. He reevaluates his life and his priorities, and becomes a husband and a father to two beautiful children. For the first time in his life he is living for others, when suddenly, BAM!—he gets cancer! No, not now, he is so close, he's worked so hard! He has a family that depends on him! In an act of desperation, he devises a plan. It's a big heist (details of heist not hashed out at this point).

Now what kind of person has these thoughts at a time like this, a man who is deeply in love with his family and life. Or, maybe producer Vince Gilligan, who came up with a similar scenario for his hit TV series *Breaking Bad*. I decide this is not a good time for a potential plagiarism lawsuit, so I'd better focus on the matter at hand—kicking Cancer's ass!

I'm at Coffee Bean on a break in between clients, when Katie calls. She sounds almost breathless as she begins to share information with me. She's been researching "radical prostatectomy" on the Internet, and found some surgery options. The leading and most promising-sounding is robotics surgery. She also spoke to her friend (I'll call her Karen), who happens to know someone who recently had a robotics prostatectomy. Karen is a physical therapist and has a friend who specializes in rehab for prostate surgery, and just happens to work at Kaiser two days a week. Go Katie! My girl is rockin' it! Tell me more!

As Katie excitedly continues, the conversation quickly takes a scary turn. As I'm standing in line, Katie begins to tell me about the post-surgical side effects, which include incontinence and impotence. I can expect to wear a catheter. *A catheter? For how long*? She can't answer. I'm suddenly terrified and forget what I'm about to order. I'm imagining myself saying to the person behind me, "You can go ahead of me, my pee bag is full. I need to go empty it."

I have to step out of line. I'm freaking out. Still on the phone with Katie, I start to pace the floor of Coffee Bean, walking around and between people trying to keep my voice down. Abruptly I say, "Listen, please do me a favor— I don't want any more information until we understand what my particular case is. Each case is different. Let's just wait until we find out what stage my cancer is." I can hear the hurt in her voice as she replies, "Sorry, I'm just trying to help." "I appreciate it, but it's some scary shit that I don't even want to think about right now."

I was a little harsh, but my mind really can't even process all of this at once. I have a simple mind, anyway, and too much information at once could cause it to short circuit. After we hang up, I order a coffee and find a seat. I had brought my laptop to do some research on prostate cancer, but now I'm too afraid of what I might find. I just sit and stare. The Coffee Bean is busy. Is it my imagination, or is everyone here in an extra good mood today? I wonder how many people here have any trace of cancer in their body, and they have no idea.

Even though I ask Katie not to tell me any more news unless it's good, she continues to do research on her own. I decide to tell just a few people, with my mom being the first. She is a very soft-spoken, unassertive, humble woman. I know she will be shaken. I call her and we chat about the kids and life, before I ask her if she knows what PSA levels are. She doesn't. I try to break the news to her as gently as possible, and reassure her, even though I wasn't sure of much myself. I ask her to tell my sisters, but to please warn them that I don't want anyone calling me with anything they've heard about prostate cancer. I know they will be just trying to help, but I'm already freaking out. The few people who do know my diagnosis are very sweet and helpful. We begin to get numbers of people to call that who have experience and educated knowledge of prostate cancer. I speak to Katie's friend, Karen, the physical therapist. She has spoken to her friend who had radical prostatectomy robotics surgery in December. I also speak to a well-known pathologist, who recommended robotics surgery! ROBOTICS! It was a newer type of surgery where the surgeon uses a robot to perform the surgery, with the nerves being magnified on a computer screen. Sounds very interesting! The nerves being magnified means the doctor can see them better, which means there is a better chance of sparing them from damage. We need to spare these nerves!

During the coming week, I speak to Karen's friend, Brian, who had the robotics surgery. He sounds pretty upbeat. He has high praises for his surgeon, Dr. Chuang, a Kaiser surgeon located in Irvine, although he told me the surgery is performed in Downey, about 40 miles from where we live. I learn that only two Kaiser hospitals in Southern California have this robot. I also learn that the patient must be approved, but Brian tells me that I should be a good candidate. He says they prefer young and healthy cancer patients because it's such an expensive operation. I guess they don't want to use this $2.5 million dollar robot on a patient who only has a few years left. "Here ya go, Pops— try these chemo pellets or a few rounds of radiation. That should buy you a few years!" Damn you, insurance system!

Katie hustles again and gets me an appointment with Dr. Chuang in Irvine. In the meantime, I receive an email from one of my clients and producing partners, Arleen Sorkin (actress and wife of Chris Lloyd, co-creator of the hit ABC television series *Modern Family*). She has attached an email message from a friend of hers, a "very respected doctor by the name of David Agus. He is the man Sumner Redstone and philanthropist Michael Milken had hired to head up the Prostate Cancer Foundation, which Milken founded years earlier. He is also well known as Lance Armstrong's oncologist. Arleen had emailed him about me, and he had replied. Dr. Agus strongly suggested I reach out to Dr. Kaswick or Dr. Stephen Williams at Kaiser, and to use his name! *OK, let's find them!*

Katie searches the Kaiser physicians directory, but can't find any contact information for Dr. Williams. I finally locate and leave a message with a nurse for Dr. Kaswick,, but I never hear back from him. Katie continues to hustle. She gets permission to access my Kaiser profile and gets me an appointment with Dr. Chuang in Irvine. She knocks it out of the park again!

Appointment with Dr. Chuang
January 20

I'm up and out the door alone for my long and scary drive to Irvine. Katie really wanted to come, but we didn't have a sitter for Colin and she is still nursing Faith. I give myself two hours to get there and arrive with two minutes to spare. I rush to check in and hurry to the second floor, where I am directed to go. I have to make a quick stop in the bathroom first, my stomach has been messed up since the biopsy. As soon I finish my business, I rush to the waiting area without even time to sit before the nurse calls my name. *Whew! Close one!*

Dr. Chuang enters. After our introduction, he sits in front of his computer monitor, ready to get down to business. First I ask him if we can get Katie on the speaker phone. He is hesitant, but I persist, because I promised her. She has more questions than me. Before we start, I show him a picture of Katie, myself and our two little ones. I have to get approved for this surgery, so I try for the sympathy vote. He makes a casual, complimentary comment, but doesn't really look closely at the picture. I was expecting something like, "Beautiful family! You're so young

34

to have this. I will save you," followed by a "Don't worry, my child," even though we look about the same age.

Instead, he starts off with the usual questions— "Any history of prostate cancer in your family?" and so on. I tell him about my checkup two years earlier, and how that doctor didn't check my PSA level. Dr. Chuang confirms my suspicion—yes, I had cancer two years ago! He also comments about how the standard age for prostate exams in the past, started at age 50. He tells me that if I had waited until then, it would have been too late. *Wow, let's get this stuff out of my body!* Katie starts off with the scariest question of all—the survival rate. Damn, I don't want to even think about that, but she is much more realistic and practical than I am. The doctor answers that we won't know until after the surgery. Although my lab reports from the biopsy show that I have 30 percent cancer on the left side, I could have more. Katie asks when we will know if I have been approved, and Dr. Chuang replies that decision is his. I suddenly sit up straight with anticipation. Did I hear him correctly? The decision is his? *What do you want, Doc? Anything, just name it! A song and dance?* but before I jump on the table and give an *American Idol* worthy performance of "Dr. Feelgood," he glances at his computer screen and says, "I can do your surgery." I'm approved!

"All right, how's tomorrow afternoon for you, Doc?" I ask. He says he will email me by the end of the day with some possible dates. I'll take them—any of them! As promised, Dr. Chuang emails that evening with four possible dates— two in February and two in March. Katie and I discuss our options. We both have birthdays in the middle of February. Okay, it won't be the most fun birthday, but what's a better gift than life?

What was really on my mind was that I was supposed to pitch the show I have been working on, to networks in February. I had signed with Scout Productions a year-and-a-half earlier with a project that is based on the DVD that I created, *Rockstars of Comedy*. I have spent seven years working on *Rockstars*—a lot of blood, sweat and stress. Hell, maybe the stress is what caused my cancer!

I was excited to sign with Scout because they had created successful television shows in the past and had many Emmy Awards. I want some of those! Our plan was to attach a known rock star before we pitch to networks. Our number one choice was Tommy Lee. Tommy had already passed on the project about a year earlier, so we were looking elsewhere when his manager reached out to Scout. We had the band Camp Freddy on board as our house band. Camp Freddy is comprised of Dave Navarro, along with an interchanging line-up of rock stars, usually including members of Guns N' Roses, The Cult and Ozzy's band. Pretty damn cool! Camp Freddy's manager also represented Tommy. He called over to Scout and wondered why we hadn't offer the host gig to Tommy? We said we had offered it to him, but he passed! About a month later, after some contract negotiations, Tommy was signed. It was time to rock.

This was a tough call. Do I risk carrying the cancer creeping around in my body for another month, or do I go in and get this over with ASAP? After much discussion with Katie, I decide to hold off the operation until March 1st. I really needed to sell *Rockstars of Comedy* for the future security of my family, and my sanity. However, by the time I called Dr. Chuang's office the next day, the March 1st date was taken, as well as the mid-February date. Now the only options are the beginning of February or March 24th. I am nervous to wait that long, but I decide to take the March date anyway. I also decide not to tell Scout Productions about my cancer. I can't let them see a chink in my armor. I need to go into these meetings like a rock star, and rock stars are invincible! If the networks knew I had cancer, they may question whether I will be around to produce this show.

During this time, Katie and I are begin to receive lots of messages from family and friends (mostly hers) expressing concern and offering prayers. I have been on my own most of my life, so I've always found it difficult to accept help from anyone. However, this outpouring of love really touched me. Damn, I'm so lucky that I have Katie in my life!

I decide to call my buddy, Dr. Ken Jeong. He is the Asian guy in the movie *The Hangover* who jumps out of the trunk naked. I've known him for over 10 years through stand-up comedy. Believe it or not, Ken was actually a doctor at Kaiser. I would assume when Ken told his parents that he was going to quit being a doctor to tell jokes, they weren't too happy, but now that his acting career has taken off, all is forgiven! Ken's wife, Tran, is also a doctor at Kaiser. She was diagnosed with breast cancer several years ago, so I know that not only could Ken give me sound advice as a friend and doctor, but he has personal experience with the C-word. Just as I thought, Ken was a great help. I had told him that although I was grateful Dr. BSM originally found the cancer, I didn't feel comfortable with the thought of him cutting me open. I told Ken about Dr. Chuang and the other two surgeons I was trying to reach. He told me to go with my gut instinct and fuck hurting anyone's feelings, because it's MY life on the line. He went on to tell me that one of his good friends was supposed to operate on his wife, but they decided to go with someone else. Good advice, my friend! Dr. BSM, looks like you'll have time to go ahead and play that back nine, because you won't be operating on me.

To Ken's wife, Tran, I wish you a long and healthy life with Ken and your beautiful twin daughters. To Ken, thanks for the advice. But please don't jump out of any more trunks nude. My retinas are still damaged from seeing that!

5

Born to Lose

It was a cold, dreary winter morning on January 1, 1982. Uncle Melvin, my mom's oldest brother, had just dropped my friend Dale and me off at my house. My dad had had a few friends over the night before to ring in the New Year and to celebrate his birthday. He had just turned 40 on December 22. I had volunteered to stay at Uncle Melvin's so Dad could enjoy himself with other grownups. After a few knocks (I had forgotten my keys) Dad answered the door. I don't remember him saying much, but I do remember that he was wearing his robe, and he looked like hell. His bedroom was next to the kitchen, so you had to pass it to walk down the hall. He walked right into his room, sat at the edge of the bed and placed his head in his hands. Dale and I stopped to look into his room as I joked, "What's wrong, Dad, got a hangover?"

He groaned "Yeah," and lit a cigarette as Dale and I laughed and went on our way to my room. After I dropped my stuff, I told Dad that I needed to give Dale a ride home on my moped (We were both 15 and didn't have our driver's licenses yet, and was illegal to drive a moped without one.) I said I would be right back. Dale lived about 5 or 6 miles away, in a much nicer neighborhood. Lately my dad hadn't been himself. He was working as a custodian at one of the two hospitals in Owensboro. I was secretly embarrassed because the father of one of my best friends was the administrator there. Dad would occasionally tell me when he would bump into someone we knew, and I would think to myself, *"Damn, you used to be this bad ass, and now you have a mop in your hand."*

My dad had been an electrician, a lineman and a few other things, but then he was in a bad accident (or shall I say, incident) while working with his brother at an electric company. He and his brother, my Uncle Harley, were high up above the ground, working a telephone pole while sharing the same bucket. My Uncle Harley was an ex-con whom my dad and others had warned me to stay away from. Dad had beaten his ass a few times in the past when Harley needed to be put in check. Uncle Harley confirmed this and even shared a few of those stories with me later. Anyway, I guess they were at it again and somehow they both fell– or pushed each other – out of the bucket, and plummeted to ground. I don't know how many feet they fell, but I assume it was pretty far. Apparently my dad landed on a sledge hammer and shattered his arm, and Uncle Harley received only minor injuries. Dad had numerous operations after the fall, but he was never able to straighten that arm again. I believe that fall also crushed his spirit. My dad had recently received a very modest settlement of approximately $30,000, and it had allowed him to buy us a small, old house. Yes, you could buy houses in bad neighborhoods in Kentucky for that amount in 1982. Maybe even now!

Dad had recently told me that most days at the hospital he would just find an empty stairwell and sleep. My dad was known around town as a hell raiser, womanizer and fun guy in his younger days. I mostly remember him being a jack of all trades, and master of none. He could sing, play the guitar and piano, he knew pool tricks and cards tricks. He could even walk on his hands. I've since come to the conclusion that most of these talents were the result of a misspent youth. I always knew he was fun and generous, although I heard you did not want to get on his bad side, especially if he had a couple of drinks in him. Usually when I go home to visit now, it seems another person has a story about how my dad kicked somebody's ass.

Example: One 4th of July when my parents were still married, the city was having a fireworks show down by the river, and the authorities decided to let the prisoners out to enjoy the show. Good intentions, but very bad logistics! The jail is about a block from the river, so they loaded up the prisoners in the police vans and took these nice, deserving gentlemen down there. The police were unloading the prisoners, when one inmate decided to attack a cop. He was a large man with a long criminal record. The story in the paper reported that he was beating and biting Officer David Bradley, and had removed his handgun. Now, there must've been over a thousand spectators in the crowd watching, but no one was coming to the rescue to save this man, except for my dad, Sherman Dupin. Dad was an electrician at the time, and happened to be around the area in his work van when he saw the incident taking place. He jumped in and gave the prisoner a proper beat-down and restrained him until some back-up arrived. I would imagine the inmate wasn't too pleased with my dad interfering, and botching his ingenius escape plan: beat and bite cop, take gun, possibly shoot cop and anyone else who gets in the way! The story goes that it took 20 minutes or more for police to arrive and get this guy into custody.

A couple of days later, my dad arrived home from work, and my mom informed him that he needed to down to the police station to fill out some paperwork regarding the incident. When they arrived at the police station, the local newspaper was there, as well as the officer whose life my dad had saved, to present my dad with a plaque for "Outstanding Bravery." I'm sure this was the first time my dad had ever been commended for anything by law enforcement. My dad used this credit, and milked it for all he could.

For example: I have a vague memory of a high-speed chase involving my dad, his girlfriend Mary, and me. Dad was driving a black Karmen Ghia, and had many police cars chasing him. I don't quite remember why they were chasing us. It must've involved an attempt to pull him over for suspicion of DUI. I remember Mary crying and begging my dad to stop. "Sherman," she shouted. "Please, if you love me, you will stop this car!" Well, that should've answered her question!

Dad kept up this chase, with a hell raiser's abandon! Instead of looking terrified, I remember how he almost seemed delighted at the challenge. We came upon a roadblock the police had made by lining several patrol cars bumper-to-bumper across the road. My dad did one of those cool moves you see in movies with high-speed car chases, where he went up an embankment on one side of the road, kept the pedal to the metal and sped away! *(That was some cool shit Dad, even though you could've just killed your son and what's her name...Mary!)* We made it back to their trailer, with many cop cars in tow.

When we got out of the Karman Ghia, there was mayhem. Lots of police were yelling and trying to move toward my dad, as he remained calm and and continued to taunt them. "I will kick everybody's ass here!" he shouted. (Reality check: High-speed chases aren't like you saw on *Dukes of Hazard*, where those crazy Duke boys would beat sheriff Roscoe P. Coletrain home after a wild, high-flying chase, and he would say something like, "Ah shucks, we'll get dem Duke boys next time.")

One particular officer knew my dad (or knew of him), and began trying to plead with him. I just remember my dad saying something like, "You guys can take me, but if *that* son of a bitch touches me, there's going to be a lot of trouble and ass-whoopings." I have no idea which officer he was referring to was, or about his history with my dad, but the officer in charge agreed, and they took my dad away without a fight after agreeing to *his* terms. Next thing I remember is Mary attempting to call my mom, but passing out in mid-conversation. I took the phone and told my mom Mary was asleep and the police took Daddy. Shortly thereafter, my mom arrived at the police station with my grandmother (my dad's mom), and they took me home.

It was around 2:00 p.m. when I arrived home from taking Dale home. Dale and I had gotten got caught up watching a couple of boxing matches, and I won two dollars off of him. "This is my lucky day!" I shouted. As I walked through the back door into the kitchen of my house, I noticed half-melted ice cubes in the kitchen sink. Apparently dad had just dumped his ice from one of his many Diet Cokes of the day. I called his name, but there was no answer. I began to look around, inside the house and then outside and in the garage. His car was there, along with his motorcycle. Dad dated a woman, Wanda, who lived a few blocks away, so I thought maybe he had gone somewhere with her, but it was very odd for him not to leave a note.

It was about two hours before the phone rang. It was Donald Victors, an ex-con and friend from my dad's hell-raising years. Dad had recently given Donald $200 so his kids could have Christmas. Donald asked if I was alright. *Weird question*, I thought. I answered "Yes, why?" There was a pause and he asked if I was home alone, and I said yes. He sounded calm, but very concerned, and he said he would be right over. As I hung up, I began to get an eerie chill. *What the F?* Within a few minutes, the phone rang again, and as I picked it up I heard what I believed was crying. It was one of Wanda's kids. I heard her take the phone away from her ear without saying a word to me, and saying "Mom, he's there!" Wanda got on the phone and said, "Honey, don't leave, I'll be right there!"

As I hung up, I started to panic, "No, no, no! What the fuck is going on?" The room was spinning. I decided to call the emergency room at Daviess County Hospital (which was also where Dad worked). I asked the lady who answered, "Can you please tell me if Sherman Dupin has been in there today?" She said she couldn't give that information. I explained that I was his son. "Can you please check?" I asked. I could hear her cover the phone with her hand as she spoke to a man. She said something to the effect of, "I have this patient's son on the phone and he's asking if his dad has been in!"

She came back and said in a very hesitant voice, "Yes, there has been a Sherman Dupin in." *Has been?* My heart was pounding! What does that mean— *"been in?"* She came back on and asked if I was alone. I said yes, and I heard her tell the other guy, "He's home all alone." At this point the male got on the phone and I knew what he was about to say. I did not want a complete fucking stranger dismissively tell me my father had died over the phone, so I hung up! I began to run around the house screaming and crying, "No! Please, God, no! He's all I've got!"

A few minutes later Wanda walked in. I also *did not* want to hear the news from his most recent fling, but before I could get away she said, "Honey he's gone!" I told her that she was lying as she tried to console me. Holding me and telling me how much he loved me, how much we loved him, blah, blah, as I just kept telling her to shut up. "You're lying!" I said. My skin was crawling. I had to get the hell out of there. I ran out of the house and jumped on my moped. It must've been in the low 30s outside; there was still snow and ice on the ground. I rode about five miles to a secluded area in the woods, next to a creek. I sat there crying for hours in the freezing cold. I had nowhere else to go. When I finally returned to my house, it was full of relatives. I didn't want to see, touch or hear anyone, even though I knew they were all just trying to help. I ran in my room and threw myself face down on the bed. My relatives started to file into my room, each with condolences and suggestions. A couple of them offered to let me come and live with them, which I appreciated, but I couldn't wrap my head around any of it. I had just seen my dad earlier in the day, and now my whole world was turned upside-down! I just wanted to be alone.

I don't recall much after that, until the private viewing of the body. I walked in right behind my grandmother (we all called her Mother). She had been remarried to a nice man for years. I don't remember if my dad's father was there the first night. His name was Harley Dupin, Sr. I had only seen him a few times growing up. I didn't know much about him, other than he was a veteran and an alcoholic. Those few times that I had been to see him, he was always wearing a wife beater and smelled like booze. My grandparents had divorced when my dad was a teenager. After that, my dad began his years of hell-raising. He dropped out of school in the 10th grade. He had no plan, so he lied about his age and joined the Army. He later received a dishonorable discharge for fighting. When Dad was an adult he decided to have all of the tattoos on his arms removed. This was years before laser removal surgery existed, so he had them burned off. He only left one tattoo remaining on his upper left arm that read, "Born to Lose."

As we walked into the viewing room, my grandmother took one look at my dad lying in the coffin and screamed, "Ooh, God no, my baby!" She passed out and hit the ground.

I had a half-brother from Arizona that who was there, as well as my half-brother Gary, who had grown up in Louisville. I had only seen the one from Arizona a couple of times in my life, but I had seen Gary more as a child, before my parents divorced. There are lots of pictures of the two of us together. Gary had recently moved to Owensboro, but my dad and he weren't close. I believe my dad thought he would be a bad influence on me, so Gary wasn't invited over much. Gary told me he had learned of our dad dying from reading the obituaries in the newspaper, while sitting in jail. Gary died about 10 years later when he was struck in the back of the head with a tire iron in a fight.

It was extremely cold the day of the funeral. I just remember crying and shaking uncontrollably. As we were driving away, I kept looking back to see if the workers were really going to place him in the ground. I was still in a state of shock and disbelief. When I got home I just thought, *now what?* My grandmother was the executor of the estate, so I knew she would be selling the house soon. I didn't want to go back home to Mom and her abusive husband. Fortunately, my Uncle Harley was granted temporary custody of me.

6

On a Lighter Note

Sorry if I bummed you out with that last story. Let's kick this chapter off with something a little lighter: my crazy friend, Dale. I met Dale while attending Daviess County Middle School, after we moved to a brand new government housing apartment across town. I didn't know anyone on the other side of town, until this crazy character came along. Dale was hilarious and a complete maniac. Unlike me, Dale's family was middle to upper middle class. His father, a construction foreman, seemed to tolerate us, but never really paid much attention. His mom was a beautiful, athletic brunette (a MILF before the term was invented). Dale also had a half-brother who was very fit, good-looking and a few years older than us. Dale took great joy in fucking with everyone, even his older, stronger brother. His brother would sit at the piano and play, very beautifully and methodically. And then it would be Dale's turn to sit and play. Immediately his brother would start to get tense, and warn him not to bang on the keys. Dale would have his usual mischievous grin on his face as he began to play, softly at first, and then, leaning forward with his face close to the keys, and like a deranged Jerry Lee Lewis, he would start free-styling some crazy made-up song. As the tempo got faster, he would bang harder and harder! Meanwhile his brother would be pacing in and out of the room, screaming his head off for him to stop! Now I would be laughing nervously because it was hysterical, but at the same time I was thinking, *Why would you do this, when you know you are about to get pummeled?* Dale couldn't help himself, and soon enough his brother would rip him off the bench and start chasing him around the house, dishing out a beat-down. Dale would half-pretend to fight back, but mostly just yell and exaggerate the pain being dealt, which would infuriate his brother even more. Finally, his brother would just get tired of beating him and storm off ranting about what an idiot Dale was. Now, why would Dale do this time and time again, knowing the consequences? Because it was funny.

Rough River, Kentucky

A couple of years later, when I was around 14, Dale, another guy that I didn't know very well named Greg, and I went camping at a place called Rough River, Kentucky. Rough River State Resort Park was an outdoor area with fishing, tube riding, camping and a small lodge. It was a conservative family retreat in a dry county (where alcohol is illegal). Now, you understand why moonshine is still made in Kentucky.

Dale's cool, attractive mom checked us in and helped find our little designated spot for our tent. Meanwhile, I was wishing she would throw on some Daisy Dukes so I could pitch my own tent. *Ba dum bum!* We each had a sleeping bag, a little food, lots of Little Debbie® cakes (a Southern delicacy), and some other contraband.

After his mom warned us to stay out of trouble and have fun (isn't that an oxymoron?), she left us there with instructions where, and when, she would pick us up the next day, if we lasted that long.

Within just a few minutes after she left, we decided to hit the lodge and check out the families with teenage girls checking in. It was around noon and a lot of people were checking in. We moseyed over to the couches to get a good view of things. It was a typical-looking lodge with a stone fireplace, some faux leather couches, and out-of-date chairs overlooking the beautiful Kentucky landscape. We were kicking back and goofing around when Dale said he was going to light up a joint. *Light a what?* Greg and I pleaded with Dale, "Man, are you crazy? Don't fuck around; we're going to get arrested!" Besides being highly illegal, we reminded him this was a dry county, and a family place! Dale had that mischievous grin on his face again as he reached into his pocket. *Here we go!*

By the time Dale was taking his second toke, Greg and I were heading toward a back door with a wraparound patio just outside of the huge glass windows. Within just a couple of minutes the place was wreaking of pot! We were outside where Dale could see us and we could see him, as we motioned and pleaded for him to stop! I finally ran in for a second to try and talk him out of it, or hit him over the head with a fire poker. Dale casually laughed as he snuffed out the joint and put it away. Dale was like a delinquent Ferris Bueller. I felt stares and overheard remarks as I headed back outside with Dale following. Obviously, someone did notice the smell, because two security guards—not the professional gun-toting type, but small local college dudes making a few bucks on the weekends—approached us. They said there had been a report of some teenagers smoking pot in the lodge, and did we know anything about it? "Huh? Hell, no! That stuff is illegal! We've never even seen pot!" However, we did have a few Swisher Sweets cigars on us, which Dale now lit up to prove. *Someone must've mistaken this for that illegal marijuana you speak of,* we told the guards. One of the security guys ordered us to hand it over. Dale snuffed out the one he had lit and reached into his pocket and handed the guy the box with the rest. The guy started sniffing the box, and handled it to the other as they continued to warn us about this being a dry county, and reminding us that marijuana was illegal and dangerous. It could make us hallucinate, they said, and cause harm to us or others. These guys had seen one too many *Afterschool Specials*. They finally let us go with a warning that they would be keeping an eye on us!

Greg and I were furious at Dale, but it was par for the course, so on to the next adventure! That night, as we were devouring our delicious and very un-nutritional Little Debbie cakes, Dale announced his party plan for the evening. Uh, oh! With joy in his eyes he proclaimed, "The first one that falls asleep tonight, I going to take out my dick and rub it on your mouth!" Dale looked at me with that grin and a wink, like, "I'm just fucking with you!" I picked up on it, but this was Greg's first time at the dance!

He was livid and shouted, "Bullshit! That's not funny!"

Dale kept it up, "Well, you'd better not fall asleep first then!"

Greg was getting angrier, "I'm not kidding, you'd better not fuck around!"

Now, there were many other tents with families in very close proximity to us, who had come in for a peaceful retreat. That had no idea that they would be sharing a campsite with the hillbilly spawn of Satan. After everyone had put out their campfires and lanterns, things started to get very quiet. We settled into our tent and talked about girls, girls and more girls, while relaxing. "Is that a yawn I see, Greg?" Sure enough, Greg was the first to fall asleep. Uh, oh! Now I knew Dale wasn't really going to put his dick on Greg's lips, but Greg didn't know that! So while Greg was snoozing away, Dale said "Hey, I'm going to kneel over Greg and pretend to be putting my dick back in my pants, and we will wake him."

"Oh my God," I'm thinking, *"Another classic,"* as Dale did just that! As Dale was pretending to put his dick back in his pants, and zip them up, he start yelling at Greg, "Oh, my god, I just put my dick all over your mouth!"

Greg immediately woke up in a daze, "Huh, what, what?" And then he started to come around, "You motherfucker!"

Dale kept teasing him, "You liked it! You started licking your lips!" I had never seen someone so angry in my life!

"I'm going to fucking kill you!" shouted Greg. Just then Greg grabbed a steak knife and lunged at Dale as we were both struggling to unzip the tent and get the hell out of there! Greg chased Dale around the campsite shouting, "I'm going to fucking kill you, motherfucker!" while I followed close behind, pleading with him not to do it!

"He didn't really put his dick on your mouth! You didn't lick your lips!" I shouted. By this time, other tent lights started to come on, and dads were starting to emerge, wondering what the hell was going on. Finally, after a few laps around the camping area, we finally got Greg calmed down and back into our tent! Greg didn't sleep the rest of that night and miraculously, we weren't arrested.

I didn't see much of Dale after my dad died. I had moved back across town and we were attending different high schools. Dale was in a really bad car accident when we were 17 years old. He struck a tree and went through the windshield. I took him Little Debbie cakes at the hospital. I only saw him one more time before I left Owensboro. I had my own apartment my senior year of high school (more about that den of sin, later). Dale dropped by one night for a few beers. His actions and speech were different, like he was in slow motion. But he still had his mischievous grin. I expected him to snap out of it at any minute and say, "I'm just fucking with you," but he didn't.

Hope you're still making 'em laugh, where ever you are, buddy!

7

Kegel muscles?
I didn't know men had those!

I have a phone conversation with Dave K. (name has been changed), a physical therapist who was recommended by Karen,, Katie's friend. He's very helpful, explaining the types of exercises that he teaches to help with incontinence following a prostatectomy. We set up an appointment at Kaiser Hollywood where he works two days a week. Meanwhile, Katie and I are still trying to track down Dr. Kaswick and Dr. Williams, when I find out that none other than Dr. Williams practices at Kaiser Hollywood. Bingo!

Dave seems very knowledgeable, but I'm more concerned about who will perform the surgery than I am about pissing in my pants. I need to get to the man himself, Dr. Williams. Upon learning this new information, I decide it's time for a covert operation— some *Mission: Impossible*-type shit! My goal is to go to my appointment, get chummy with Dave, and then work him to get some info about Dr. Williams. If he doesn't know anything, I will have to take matters into my own hands and stalk Dr. Williams (cue *Psycho* music here).

January 28

Before I leave my house the morning of my appointment with Dave, I see on the news that the nurses at Kaiser Hollywood have walked out, and are now on strike. You've got to be f-ing kidding me! Well, shit, looks like I will be busting through a picket line today! Nothing will stop me; I'll be dropped in by helicopter, if necessary! I have a long drive, but make it on time to my appointment. Actually, I didn't see any nurses striking at all. Maybe they're on the inside and have taken Dr. Williams hostage? *Don't worry, Dr. Williams, I'll bust you out of here, and I've got some experience with high-speed chases!* I enter the hospital and everything seems normal, except for some construction going on. Or, maybe it's destruction, caused by the nurses? In any case, on with my game plan: get in, act very interested in these pelvic floor exercises (or butt squeezes, or whatever), then get to Dr. Williams!

As I approach the elevator, I begin to get that feeling that's been all too familiar lately— damn, my stomach is acting up again! I've been having "movements" two or three times a day since the biopsy. Now, I'm usually very weird about going number 2 in public, but this is an emergency — I have no choice. After I finish my annihilation in the bathroom, I try to slink out as quickly as possible. Good Lord, if the nurses aren't on strike yet, they will be if they get a waft of that stench! I'm now freaking out. What if Dave has to examine me? No, I tell myself, he'll probably just talk to me and show a couple charts, give me a brochure, and we'll set up our post-surgery appointment. I've spoken to this guy on the phone. He knows my wife's friend, Karen. this should be very informal. Unfortunately for me, that wasn't the case.

I find the right department and check-in, only to find out this visit is not covered by my insurance. Apparently, they'll cover the plumbing being ripped out, but the consequential leakage that follows is my problem. About 15 minutes pass when a tall, youngish and conservative-looking guy approaches and introduces himself as Dave. I would feel much better if he was an old codger. As Dave and I make small talk, he leads me down a hall and into a room. I subconsciously tell myself that my plan is working. We've got a good rapport going here, I'll hopefully get some valuable information on Dr. Williams, and Dave will never know about the devastation I had just caused in the bathroom. However, to my shock and surprise, Dave casually instructs me to take off my pants and underwear and gives me a sheet for cover. As he walks out of the room, I'm thinking, "This was not in my plan!" I begin to try and calm myself down. *Ok, he's just going to come in and explain the exercises, and I will do them privately under this sheet.* Wrong!

Dave returns and explains that we are going to work the Kegel muscle. Huh, I didn't even know guys had one? Dan explains how to properly engage and squeeze the Kegel without moving the butt cheeks! And the best part of this sphincter party is that Dave has stuck his head under the sheet to stare at my anus to make sure I do it properly! Now what exactly is the purpose of the sheet again? Is it so I won't have to see the look of disgust on Dave's face? This is exactly the moment when I decide I'm never going to see Dave again after this appointment!

I continue to concentrate on "engaging" while Dave comes up to explain another exercise and probably to get some fresh air! Finally he steps out so I can get dressed, which I find amusing since he just had his head between my butt cheeks. When he comes back into the room, I no longer feel like casual chit-chat. I want him to forget that my wife knows Karen and even to forget he ever met me! OK, it's time to bring up Dr.Kaswick and especially Dr. Williams. After some prodding, he tells me that Dr. Kaswick is pretty much retired, and does not do robotics. OK, so Dr. Kaswick just got scratched off of my very short list. He then tells me that he personally knows Dr. Williams.

"Huh, you know him?," I ask. "Where is he? Let's go get him right now!"

Dave then informs me that Dr. Williams no longer works in Hollywood, and is now in Riverside. Riverside! That's far, but I don't care.

"Can I have his number, his email, his home address, anything?" I tell him that Dr. Agus referred me, and that I'm supposed to use his name. Dave tells me to give him my email address and that he will send him a message. I write down my email address and spell the message out very clearly: "R-e-f-e-r-r-e-d b-y D-r. A-g-u-s!" I make sure Dave can read every letter before I leave. I thank Dave and I'm out the door. Even though Dave is a professional, I feel humiliated again!

I check my Kaiser email and personal emails for 48 hours and no word. I almost give up when I receive a phone call a few days later. It's Dr. Williams' office calling to set up an appointment! Yeah, baby! It was well worth having a man stare at my filthy anus to get this invaluable appointment, although I still never want to see Dave again. Ever!

8

That's not your prostate, hillbilly!

The great thing about Facebook is that old acquaintances can reconnect, and the bad thing about Facebook is that old acquaintances can reconnect. Over the past couple of years, a lot of old friends from my hometown, many of whom I haven't spoken to since high school or earlier, have found me on there. It seems a lot of these messages include stories of some of my antics. Recent stories recounted by some of these old friends involve me crashing cars, getting a DUI on a moped, peeing on someone, and shooting arrows into a department store sign. Just the usual, innocent-kid stuff, right? Hey, I grew up in Kentucky – not a lot of entertainment there, so we had to create our own. One of these recently unearthed memories involved a very sharp No. 2 pencil…

I was in the 10th grade at Apollo High School. My third-period class was about to begin and we were all filing into the classroom. I saw a buddy of mine, Jeff Collins, talking with a female classmate, so I decided to sneak up on him and jump on his back. Fourteen-year-old boys do this a lot for no apparent reason, at least among *my* friends. I surprised Jeff with my amazing Tarzan-like leap. Good for a few seconds of laughter, then the bell rang. It was time for class. As I released my grip on his neck, and slid down his back, I heard two snaps and immediately felt a sharp, piercing pain in my groin.

"Oh, shit," said Jeff. "Dude, I had two brand-new sharpened pencils in my back pocket!" Doubling over in pain I look down at my crotch, wondering what the F just happened, when I noticed two pencils broken in half and sticking out of the crotch of my pants! *Oh, shit, I just got stabbed in the nuts!* By this time a couple of other students were gathering around. Without much thought, I reached down and attempted to pull the pencils out. One pencil came out without a problem; it didn't seem to have penetrated the jewels. *Whew!* But as I attempted to pull the second pencil out, I had to tug harder. *Uh, oh, this can't be good.* I finally managed to get the second pencil out of the hole in my jeans, but upon closer inspection I noticed there was no lead in it – it had broken off! All I know is now everyone had taken their seats in class and I'm standing there wondering what in the hell to do. I take my seat very carefully, and I begin to break out in a nervous sweat. Did I mention that I was wearing very tight, straight-leg Levi's jeans? I think today they would be called skinny jeans, only with a nice 80s stone-washed effect.

I contemplated going to see the school nurse. But wait— there is no way in hell I going to let her examine my jewels, much less operate on them. Besides, I was a late developer, only standing a little over 5 feet tall, and I had not reached puberty. What if the nurse told someone? *What if she announced over the PA system, "There will be a bake sale after school today, and by the way, I just saw Steven Dupin's nuts, and he doesn't have any hair down there!" The whole school erupts into laughter…*

No F-ing way! I raise my hand, as calmly as possible, and asked permission to go to the restroom. I thought this was a better approach than freaking out and yelling, "Hey, I just got stabbed in the nuts, I need to go examine my package, be right back!" After walking very slowly to the restroom, I finally arrive and enter a stall, locking it behind me. I'm sweating and shaking as I pull down my Levi's, looking down I see blood covering the crotch of my tighty whities! Oh, my God, I *did* get stabbed in the nuts! *What am I going to do?* I pulled my underwear down for a closer look. It's so bloody, I can't really see the damage, not to mention I was starting to get woozy and bleary-eyed. The thought of even getting grazed there is enough to make a man's knees buckle.

I do a quick wash job in the sink, stuff some paper towels inside my underwear and head back to class. Now this was only the beginning of third period; I still had four more hours before I could get out of there. To make matters worse, I was an avid BMX rider, and had ridden my bike to school that day, around eight miles. Finally, 3:30 arrives and the bell rings. The school nurse didn't make any announcement about my balls, and I was out of there! It was an extra warm spring day, as I walked slowly and carefully to my bike. Have you ever felt the humidity of May in the South? You start to sweat the second you walk out the door. I got on my bike and began to pedal the long journey home. I had ridden alongside a buddy that day, and told him to go on without me, which he did. *I can't believe he did that. What happened to "no soldier left behind?" Especially one with shrapnel is his balls!*

After the longest bike ride ever, I finally made it home and headed straight into the bathroom. I passed my mom, who noticed I looked pale and weak and asked what was wrong. There was no way I was letting my mom look at my balls. That was a job for just three people: me, myself and I. I quickly entered the bathroom and locked the door. I needed hydrogen peroxide and tools. I find tweezers and finger nail clippers. Time to operate! Now, MacGyver may have been able to build a rocket with a paper clip and some duct tape, but I guarantee he wouldn't have had the nerve to perform this procedure. I pulled off my tight Levi's and my now- red underwear. I sat on the edge of the bathtub and began the delicate task of removing the lead! I saw the puncture hole, but it seemed too small to get the tweezers in there to fish around for the lead, so I decided to cut the whole bigger! My hand was shaking, as I tried to hold the clippers steady. I pinched some skin from my scrotum, and attempted to cut a slit with the nail clippers. My brain was saying "Do it," but my hand was saying "Fuck you!" I was really sweating now. Just then my mom knocked on the door and asked what was going on. *"Everything's fine, please go away!"* Lord only knows what she thought her son was doing grunting and breathing hard in the bathroom! *Couldn't the little pervert wait until he takes a shower to do that?*

On the next attempt to cut, I closed my eyes and squeezed! Blood, lots of blood, and pain followed! No stopping now— I quickly washed away some blood, and decided to grab the tweezers— *I'm going in!* I reached inside and started to try to find the lead. After a few minutes, I got a hold of it and pulled.

It came out! But as I took a closer look, I notice the lead had broken in half! Shit! When it hit my pelvic bone, the lead must have broken! *I need to go BACK in!* I feel around with my finger tips and find another piece of lead. I fish around again with the tweezers, but this piece is much smaller and takes many attempts. Finally, I get it out! *Damn, I'm now covered in sweat and feeling nauseas, but mission accomplished.* I place both pieces of lead in a sandwich bag, and take them to school the next day for bragging rights.

After recently reading this message from my old friend, I thought, "Ah, ha! I found how I got cancer!" Had I consulted a urologist while writing this book, this is the part where he would've said, "The scrotum is not located in the prostate, you dumb hillbilly." Oh, well, same neighborhood!

Wheelin' away   —J. D. Schwalm,

Steve Dupin, 15, of 802 Idaho Lane, practices some fancy ant skies and temperatures made the outdoor acti-
riding on Carol Stream Street west of Owensboro. The pleas- cially appealing Tuesday.

Riding wheelie. those Daisy Dukes shorts could not have been healthy
for the junk area. (btw, pedophiles, address included)

9

Blaze On!

I have an uncle, Ricky Deno, who's only seven years older than me. He is my mom's brother, the youngest of six children, and the black sheep of the family. Uncle Ricky resembles the late Patrick Swayze, constantly has a smile on his face, and is always up to mischief. He was also the closest thing I had to a father figure growing up. Oftentimes, Uncle Ricky took it upon himself to look after me and take me places – kind of like a juvenile delinquent babysitter. We had a lot of fun! My grandmother (Mamaw) worked in Anderson's department store downtown, back when there was a Norman Rockwell-ish charm to Owensboro. Sadly, nowadays, the mall and the Walmart Supercenter have taken its place. At the time, it was the only store with more than one level, and was the fanciest place I'd ever been in. The three levels of Anderson's had ornate decorations, and a tube system where the employees would put the money in a canister and a vacuum would shoot the contents to another department! That was the coolest thing I'd ever seen. *Beam me up, Scotty!*

There was a movie theatre around the corner where Uncle Ricky would occasionally go to see a movie, but not the ones he was supposed to be seeing. Once he was instructed to take me to see to *The Jungle Book*, but we saw Cheech and Chong's *Up in Smoke*! While other six-year-olds were singing *Bear Necessities*, I was walking around doing my best Cheech impression— "Hey, man, this joint smells like dog shit! I think it's Doberman pincher, man!" I thought I was so damn cool.

One time when I was around 10 years old, Uncle Ricky took me over to Anderson's to see Mamaw after one of our movie excursions. Most likely, he was going to hit her up for some money for cigarettes or beer. There was an area between the first and second floor that was the smoking lounge. It's where the husbands and kids would hang out and wait for the women to shop. Guys didn't follow their wives around department stores holding their purses, back then. Anyway, it was a very small area with fake leather benches and chairs, and a huge glass window through which you could look down and see the first floor shoppers. On this particular day, Uncle Ricky looked down on the shoppers and then turned and said to me, "Hey, they can't see us up here. This is one of them two-way mirrors!" *Two-way mirrors, huh?* "Hell, yeah (Uncle Ricky started most sentences with "Hell, yeah."), we can see them, but they can't see us! Look, I'll show you. I'm going to run down there and look up, and you wave to me!" Uncle Ricky sprang down the stairs in seconds and then I saw him standing in an aisle looking up as if straining his eyes to see me. I'm waving my arms, but damn, what do you know— he can't see me! When he came back up, he said, "See, I told you! Now look, let's make some faces at the people down there!"

Sounded like a devious and funny idea to me. So we made a few faces before Uncle Ricky said, "Hey, give them the middle finger!" Now, this would not be my normal behavior, especially since my mom would probably rip the finger out of my socket, but what the heck?

"Are you sure?"

Uncle Ricky smiled and reassured me. "Hell, yeah, do it!"

Well, since Uncle Ricky seemed to think this would be funny, and he was older and cooler, I wanted to be cool, too! So I started waving my middle finger at the shoppers below. *"Hey, you, fat man in the polyester orange suit, this is for you! Hey, old lady with flowers on your hat, look at this free bird!"*

Just then, I noticed a lady look up, and then another, and she tapped another. Pretty soon, a small crowd of people were looking up and pointing at us! Panic-stricken, I immediately turned to Uncle Ricky, but he wasn't next to me. As I looked around, I saw Uncle Ricky behind me, where the shoppers couldn't see him, laughing his ass off! "Hey I was just bullshitting," he said. "That's not a two-way mirror! Hell, yeah, that's some funny shit!"

The next thing I remember is a voice over the intercom, "Dora Deno (my Mamaw), report to the smoking lounge immediately!" That was the last time I remember going to a movie or to Anderson's with Uncle Ricky.

A few years later, when Uncle Ricky got his driver's license (actually, come to think of it, I'm not sure if he did have a license), he would come to my house and pick me up, and we'd drive out to the country. There would be a cooler of beer in the back seat, several loaded guns, boxes of bullets and lots of weed! When we would get a couple of miles out of town, Uncle Ricky would pull over and let me drive. At that point, I was well under the driving age, but what the hell. I remember he would always have a junky old car, which he would claim was a classic that he could sell for a lot of money. I remember the cars would usually have a couple of clever bumper stickers that said things like, "A friend in weed is a friend indeed," or "Don't drink and drive...you might spill your drink."

These cars were also manual transmissions, or "straight shifts," as we called them. I would be struggling to see over the dash and keep the car on the road, while trying to shift the gears. The car would be making an awful sound as I would battle to change gears, and Uncle Ricky would be laughing and saying, "Hell, if you can't find 'em, grind 'em!" Our destination would be anything on the side of the road that looked like it would be fun to shoot the hell out of—old bottles, refrigerators, even old cars! You haven't had fun until you've shot up an old Studebaker. I imagine some car enthusiasts finding these classic cars and thinking, damn, this would be a perfect car to restore if some rednecks hadn't shot bullets holes in it!

Uncle Ricky dabbled in matrimony a couple of times. The first time, it was to the daughter of the president of Owensboro Municipal Utilities. This girl was from a strict Catholic family, and obviously from a different side of town than where we grew up. From the start, there were a few kinks in their wedding plans, the biggest one being the fact that his wife-to-be was pregnant and it was becoming more obvious every day. The second problem—Ricky had gone on an all-night bender and had a bad car crash in the company truck on his way to work one morning. I believe the official story was that a deer had jumped in front of this truck. I personally had never seen a deer on Main Street before, but that was the story, and we stuck to it.

I remember walking down the hall toward his hospital room and smelling a strong scent of a certain herb as I approached. When I entered his room, I saw Ricky holding a small object to his lips, inhaling and then blowing smoke into a wash cloth. When I asked what he was doing, he explained, "This is a one-hitter. See, I take a hit and blow the smoke in this wash rag so nobody can smell it!"

Although Ricky wasn't scheduled for release for weeks, the doctor gave him a pass to allow him attend his wedding and reception and then return to the hospital that evening. Exceptions can be made when your father is the president of the utility company. The show must go on, especially when the bride looks like she has a basketball under her white wedding dress.

The ceremony and reception would have made an excellent episode of a reality show. On one side of the church were the bride's guests—the elite of Owensboro. On the other side were Ricky's peeps, the West End hell-raisers. I remember as the bride and groom were exchanging their vows, one of Ricky's friends shouted out, "Get some, Deno!" The bride's father must've been so proud.

Surprisingly, that blissful union only lasted a few months, but Ricky's child is still the light of his life. Some years later he gave marriage another shot. This time, in true Uncle Ricky fashion, the ceremony was conducted in the living room of his trailer, with his bulldog serving as best man.

To this day, no one has any idea what Uncle Ricky does for a living (well, actually I have some idea.), yet he's always in a hurry. At family gatherings he's always the last to arrive and the first to leave, saying, "Hell, yeah, got to get out here; got to go to work!" *Damn, Uncle Ricky you must be as rich as Donald Trump!* I've never seen anybody work so hard, without actually seeing them work.

Uncle Ricky would give you the shirt off his back. He was always laughing, especially at his own jokes. He even always had his own catch phrases, like "Blaze on!" He finished almost every sentence with "Blaze On!" When he's mad at someone, he likes to say, "I'll kill that son a bitch and skull-fuck him!" I always think, *Wouldn't that make you a homosexual necrophiliac?* but I know he really hadn't put too much thought into it.

A couple of years ago, I put a video of Uncle Ricky on YouTube. He always seems to somehow know when I visit, and he had popped in at my mom's house to say hi. I took a video of him opening his Christmas present, even though this was now Mother's Day weekend in May. No one had seen him in months. He was talking his usual hillbilly jive about being happier than a "fat girl with food stamps," and cracking himself, and everyone else, up! It was classic Uncle Ricky. "Blaze on!"

I recently got the chance to work with Tommy Chong on the set of a pilot that I was producing. I told him about Uncle Ricky, and he enjoyed hearing about his shenanigans. Tommy's wife, Shelby, who was also in the pilot, said that Tommy gets approached all the time from stoner-looking dudes telling him how much he meant to them. She laughingly said that it's never someone who went on to become a doctor. However, I suspect there may be some pharmacists who are fans.

Tommy was gracious enough to sign a picture for Uncle Ricky, and wrote "'Blaze On' Uncle Ricky" on it. I sent it to Uncle Ricky via his sister, my Aunt Anna, because no one has an actual address for him. I got a call a couple of months later from him, and he sounded ecstatic, like he had just won the lottery. "Hey, Stevie, I got that damn picture of Tommy Chong! That's cool as hell, man! Got that son of a bitch hanging right here on my wall in the liv' room." *(Glad you like it, Uncle Ricky, but you might want to take that down before your probation officer drops by.)* He went on to say something about renting a Camaro and coming out to visit me. This is something he's been saying since I lived in Florida. He also asked me to make him a "tape" with some cool music on it.

I'm convinced that Uncle Ricky could be a bigger reality star than Honey Boo Boo, but the problem is that the network would be sued weekly by politically correct crybabies. Uncle Ricky is an equal opportunity offender, but he really doesn't mean to hurt anyone. He's like a white-trash version of Don Rickles.

Uncle Ricky recently got his few minutes in the spotlight on the local news station and on the front page of the *Owensboro Messenger Inquirer*, because he was stabbed. Apparently, there was an altercation between Ricky and an acquaintance outside his house. The story he told my family was that this friend wanted to drive home, and Ricky tried to take his keys because the man was too drunk. Sounds like a reasonable story for the judge. Anyway, the man reached into his truck, grabbed a hunting knife, spun around and stabbed Ricky in the stomach. The wound was so severe, the doctors weren't sure if Ricky was going to make it. After the surgery, the doctor came out to speak to our family. He told my sister Donna that when the paramedics brought him in, he was conscious and sitting up and joking, while his guts were literally hanging out of his sliced-open stomach. That's our Uncle Ricky! I wonder if he used his one-hitter in the hospital this time? Blaze On!

Catching up with Uncle Ricky on a visit home.

10

High School Daze

High school can be scary, but attending a new high school with 1500 students is terrifying. However, something changed in me when I became a student at Apollo High School. I decided that, instead of becoming a wallflower, I was going to change my persona and become a joke-cracking, rule-breaking, white-trash pimp (who happened to be only five feet tall, with long, curly, blond hair. Yes, it was a perm.) In hindsight, I should've put studying on the agenda, also. Apollo was a nice high school in the county school system, instead of the city school system, which I had attended all but one year prior. My hometown has four high schools—one city, one Catholic, and two county schools. The city schools were filled with kids from lower-income families, the county schools with the middle class, and the Catholic school with upper-middle class kids and a few inner-city black kids who received "scholarships" to play sports. I'm still not sure how that was legal.

Anyway, the plan seemed to work. I roamed the halls cracking jokes and making new friends while terrorizing classrooms with my hijinks. Of course, I was only trying to get attention and overcompensate for my insecurities. Years of self-help analysis have taught me that. My foolish antics were duly rewarded. I was voted class president in the 10th thru 12th grades, and won the school talent shows those three consecutive years also—two years as a drummer in a band, and the final year as a break dancer (seemed like a good idea at the time). As if these rewards weren't enough to add fuel to the fire, I was also voted "Biggest Flirt." I was now *Dante's Inferno*. Throughout my senior year, during our school's pep rallies, I would hold a boom box and rap over instrumental tunes to the audience.

Might I remind you that this was 1984, four years before Vanilla Ice and long before Eminem, chick a chick a... Slim Shady. As I have said before, ignorance is bliss! I promise you if my son comes home one day and says, "Yo pops! I think I'm going to bust some rhymes at the pep rally tonight," I will proceed to bust my foot in his ass to save his dignity!

There are too many wild stories to go into here, maybe I'll save them for another book. Also there still may be outstanding warrants stemming from my behavior, so I want to play it safe.

After my dad died, I was a boy without a home. Moving back in with my mom and her abusive, dumb-ass of a husband was not an option at this time either. I was living in the house I had shared with my dad, but now with my ex-con Uncle Harley. One evening, my half-sister Sandy came over and informed me that her dad had a conversation with my dad a couple of months earlier. I had only been living with Dad a few weeks, when he came to see me on the homecoming court. Sandy's dad, Don, was also there to watch a friend's daughter. Don and my dad had been high school buddies, so while talking, my dad had asked Don if he would look out for me, if anything were to happen to him. My dad was only 39 years old at the time. Did he know something that I didn't? I will never know the answer, but it was eerie, nonetheless. Don had said he would look after me, so he offered for me to come live with him and his wife, Barbara. My sisters, Sandy and my other half-sister, Donna, had lived with them during high school, but they were now gone. I suppose it was a strange situation, but I didn't have a lot of options, so I took them up on it.

Don and Barbara went to church regularly and had even formed a gospel duo. Don was also an avid hunter, and strongly encouraged me to hunt. At this point I also received Social Security checks because my father had passed away. Don would take living expenses and buy me hunting equipment from my checks. I had no interested in getting my ass up at 4:00 a.m., driving out to the country, climbing up a tree and sitting in a cold deer stand for hours. Once, as I was sitting high up in a tree, freezing my ass off, I was sleepy, so I leaned against the trunk behind me and dozed off. I could've fallen out of that tree and broken my damn neck, but I was awakened by a crackling noise below me. I open my eyes to see a beautiful doe sniffing around (that's a female deer for you city folks). All I had to do was raise my shotgun and BAM, venison steaks for everyone. Would this be my passage into manhood? I wasn't going to find out, because I couldn't do it! I made a noise to startle her, and the skittish doe looked up at me and, in a split second, she was gone. Ted Nugent would shoot me, himself, had he seen this. I just couldn't level Bambi like that. When we got back into the truck, Don and his friend asked me if I saw anything. Of course I lied and said no.

I lasted about 15 months living at Don and Barbara's house. It was almost spring break, in my junior year of high school. I was supposed to go down to Panama City Beach, Florida, with a friend and his parents. I was so excited about this trip because I had hardly been out of the Kentucky my whole life. Something kept telling me that this trip would change my life. About two weeks before I was to go, we were having dinner one night, when Don told me that I had been acting up at school and didn't deserve to go anywhere on spring break. Of course I had been acting up at school—I was the class clown! That was my job! If he would've given me the ultimatum a few months or weeks before, I would've straightened up my act. Even though I was very grateful that Don and Barbara had taken me in, I always felt like I was living in a foster home. I had to leave. My only choice now was to go back to my mom's, which is where I went.

I did end up going to Panama City with a friend and his parents, and it did indeed change my life. When we first arrived in Panama City, it was early in the morning. We had been driving all night, so we pulled in to get some breakfast at a local cafe. I immediately jumped out of the car and ran to see the ocean. It was amazing, it was breathtaking, it was something I'd never seen before, it was....*the ocean!*

There is a big nightclub located on the beach called Spinnaker. Every day while frolicking on the beach, I would stare at this club in awe, like it was the Cinderella Castle at Disneyland. Rumor had it that a guy from Bowling Green,

Kentucky, worked there. Wow~ Someone actually got out of Kentucky and established a new life in this paradise? How did he do it? What was his magic formula? Is this my crossroads? Do I need to sell my soul to the Devil to live in this Utopia? As crazy as it sounds, I kept wanting to go into Spinnaker, meet this guy and ask him how he did it. I never did go into Spinnaker, since I was only 17. However, I started to tell my friends that I was going to move to Panama City Beach after high school and dee jay at Spinnaker. I should've had a higher goal, but at least it was a goal.

Life at my mom's house with SFB was miserable, as was to be expected. I'm sure I was far from a perfect teen, but this guy was evil incarnate. The only peace I had was when he was on the road, working as a truck driver. One afternoon my mom came home from work and warned me that SFB was on his way home and was in a particularly bad mood. She had moved my car the day before and had bumped the storage shed, causing damage. She told him about it over the phone, but apparently he didn't believe her and was convinced that I had done it! She had given me the heads-up, and I had a feeling this was going to be bad.

Sure enough, I was standing at the stove heating a can of Campbells' soup (a cheap go-to meal for poor folks), when SFB stormed into the house. He was swearing, yelling, berating my mom for trying to cover for me, when I finally interrupted and said, "I didn't hit your fucking shed, so why don't you get over it?" Apparently he wasn't going to get over it, because he immediately charged at me, and started swinging! Now, I was a skinny dude—127 pounds—but if this wife-beating piece of shit wanted to go, then let's do it! As we were slinging each other around the kitchen, I got a great shot in, while he continued trying to knee me in the balls. As the fight progressed into the living room, with fists flying, I noticed a large metal candlestick on the television. My first instinct was to grab it and smash him in the head, and I wish I had. Amazingly, during this chaos, thoughts ran through my head like, "If I seriously injure this fool, will I go to jail or to reform school? Where will I live?" I was so pissed that this fuck-up was trying to ruin my life. I pushed him against the front door, but somehow I slipped up and he got my arm behind my back. Even though I was in pain, I continued to call him every name under the sun. I think I was actually speaking in tongues at that point. I thought he would just let go and we would go on with our dysfunctional lives, but to my surprise, this fucker was really trying to break my arm!

Are you serious dude? You're really trying to break a kid's arm? Damn, why didn't I smash his head with that candlestick, when I had the chance? What I can recall next was my mom yelling that the cops were on their way. As SFB released my arm, he and I exchange more words, and I headed straight to my room and grabbed the 20-gauge shotgun my dad had given me for my 12th birthday. *I may not shoot a deer, but I WILL shoot a dumbass!* I started taunting SFB from my bedroom, calling him names like "wife beater," "pussy," "coward" and anything else I could think of. I had never been so angry in my life. He took the bait and came back to the doorway of my room, unfortunately with my mom at his side. I pointed the loaded gun right at him, and yelled for my mom to get out of the way, but she wouldn't move! Now, even though I was in a state of rage, I didn't really want to kill him. That would be too easy. My plan was to blow his fucking knees off. I wanted him to think of me with every limp that he would take for the rest of his life!

I was still yelling obscenities at this piece of shit when the police arrived. Of course, he ran right outside to them playing Mr. Good Guy, and reported to them that I pulled a gun on him for no apparent reason. What a sweetheart. He seemed to leave out the details of hitting me first and trying to break my arm. Obviously, he was hoping they would rush in with guns blazing, or at least arrest me, but this was Kentucky, and it wasn't unusual for the police to deal with domestic disputes where fire arms were involved. My mom played the usual subservient, abused wife and remained silent. The police had been to our house before with no arrest made, so once again, after a little lecture, no one was arrested and they left us to fend for ourselves. My past experience told me that my mom wasn't going anywhere, so I moved out and got my own apartment, even though I was only 17 years old. My mom signed the lease, and I used my Social Security checks to pay for rent and food. Now a 17-year-old, still in high school, should not—I repeat, *should not* have his own apartment!

My apartment became a delinquent's nightclub. We even christened it "The Crib." I soon realized that my measly four-hundred-dollars a month Social Security check wasn't going to cover my bills, so I subsidized my income with keg parties, which I threw every weekend. I would sell my party attendees a red solo cup for $5, which entitled them to unlimited beers, or as many as they could drink before the keg ran out. My senior year in high school was complete, unsupervised mayhem! Even though I was innately a good person, I began to feel angry that I was cheated out of a childhood. I started acting out, getting into a lot of trouble, getting arrested, crashing cars, etc. While all of my friends had nice families to go home to, I would go home after school and eat TV dinners and stay up way too late watching old *Dick Van Dyke Show* reruns, feeling alone. (By the way, that is still my favorite show of all time).

Even though my friends thought it was so cool that I had my own apartment, I envied them for having families. They all had plans for after high school— go to college, get married, have a family and a career. I didn't have a dream besides moving to Panama City Beach and becoming the deejay at Spinnaker Beach Club. I enrolled in college at Western Kentucky University in Bowling Green, Kentucky. I had no college fund of course, so I got qualified for some government grants. I knew I wouldn't last long, maybe a semester, but then what?

About a month before senior year was to end, my sister Sandy came over one night. She told me that her husband, who was in the Air Force, was going to be stationed at Tyndall Air Force base in Florida. She said that it would be good for me to get out of Kentucky and offered for me to come and live with them. "Where is Tyndall Air Force base?" I asked. "In Panama City," She answered. *Cha- ching! Game changer, I'm out of here!* Two weeks after I graduated from high school, Uncle Ricky and two of my friends picked me up and drove me to the Nashville airport. Of course, Uncle Ricky loaded up with plenty of booze and reefer for our road trip. I boarded a very small plane, with a single row of seats on one side, and double-seats on the other, holding about 15 passengers total. It was the first time I'd ever flown on an airplane. As we lifted off, I looked out my window and knew I would never turn back. Good bye, my Old Kentucky Home!

"Hardships often prepare ordinary people for an extraordinary destiny" -C.S. Lewis

11

Take me down to Panama City

Panama City wasn't exactly the paradise I had imagined, when I first arrived. I spent the first year with Sandy and her husband on Tyndall Air Force B ase, located on the east part of town, away from action. (I'd like to take this opportunity to apologize for the torture I put them through.) I truly appreciate them taking me in and putting up with my nonsense. I don't know where I would've ended up, if Sandy hadn't stepped in to help. Shortly after arriving, I learned that there are rules to living on an Air Force base, even for a civilian. One morning, as Sandy was driving me to class at the local community college, a car was apparently annoyed at how slow she was driving, and the other driver began to honk the horn. Of course, I turned around in my seat and proceed to give this anal-retentive ass-wipe the middle finger. Finally, as the enraged man pulled alongside us, I noticed him shouting something. I rolled down my window to hear, "You're in serious trouble with the United States Air Force!" The man, who appeared to be some sort of officer, told Sandy to pull her car over. Sandy is very conservative and soft-spoken, so this incident had her extremely anxious. As we pulled over, I was still being a defiant punk, making remarks that did not help the situation. The man approached Sandy's window and asked in a very angry tone who she was. I told him it was none of his damn business, and told her not to answer him. It was at this time that he identified himself as a lieutenant. Apparently it *was* his business. Man, some people just don't have a sense of humor.

After my brother-in-law was called into his commanding officer's office and was reprimanded, I decided I had better move out before I got him court-martialed. I moved in with an alcoholic, manic-depressive bed-wetter named Eddie. Eddie was a coworker of mine at the Camelot Music store in a shopping mall. I believe he worked as the assistant manager. I had just begun deejaying on the weekends in a local bar called Pineapple Willy's (the drinking age was 19 when I moved there). Eddie and I used to drink a lot, raise hell and over-sleep for work. I'm sure it was quite a sight to see two young drunks running through the mall to open Camelot Music, while the other stores had opened 30 minutes earlier. After the mall management fined our store several times, Eddie and I weren't allowed to open anymore. That was fine with us, because it allowed more time to sleep off hangovers.

While living with Eddie, I got a full-time job as a deejay at a local night club, Montego Bay. One evening, while I was off work, an incident occurred there that could've cost me my life. I was in the club with a girl I was dating, and we got into a heated argument. While we were shouting insults at each other, a friend of hers stepped in and threw a drink in my face. Now, I wasn't a fan of this friend, anyway, so I insulted her so badly, she's probably still crying over it. About this time, three drunken rednecks decided they were going to defend this lady (of the night). Even though I was highly inebriated, I had enough wits about me to realize that this was my place of employment, so I had better pump my brakes and head out before things got really ugly.

My girlfriend and I had ridden to the club with a friend of mine, Craig, who was around 6'2" and 120 pounds soaking wet, and definitely not looking for a fight. My girl and I continue our verbal argument as we made our way toward the car. As we started to leave, I saw the three guys with whom I had had the verbal confrontation exit the bar, and jump into their cars. As we peeled out of the parking lot, the drunken shit-kickers were hot on our trail. By the way, did I mention that my lovely pool hall queen was also a psychopath? I told Craig to just keep driving and take us to my place, while she berated me and threatened to jump out of the car. I thought I left I had left Kentucky to get away from drama and better myself, but apparently some of it had followed me to the Redneck Riviera. As Craig's Corolla tore into the apartment complex parking where Eddie and I lived, I instructed him to drop us off and get out of there. He was more than happy to oblige, but expressed concern about my safety. I told him not to worry, that I had it all under control. As I quickly exited the car, I saw the rednecks rip into the parking lot as my girlfriend and I bolted up the stairs. I entered my apartment and immediately went into Eddie's room, where he lay passed out in a drunken slumber. I started rummaging through his closet, waking him.

Rubbing his eyes to make sure he was wasn't seeing things he asked, "What are you doing man?"

"I need your .38," I said. "I have a little problem."

Eddie suddenly sat straight up in his bed and asked, "Why do you need my gun?"

Before I could answer, I found the chrome .38 right on the top shelf under his tee-shirts. I grabbed the gun and was out the door! I ran past my girlfriend, saying something to the effect of, "See what you started? Now I'm going to finish it!"

As I headed down the steps, I saw the three inbred vigilantes piling out of their car, a brownish early 80s Mustang. I held the pistol in the air and shouted, "Hey, you looking for me, you pussies?" With that, I squeezed the trigger, firing off a round into the night sky. The complex must've had at least 150 units, but all was quiet, except for this hillbilly lunatic screaming at the top of his lungs and firing a pistol. I must say I felt a strange sense of pride when I saw the Three Musketeers turn and start piling back into their car. I was so full of glee, testosterone and vodka that I fired off two more rounds into the air. It's not uncommon for men in this part of the country to carry firearms in their cars, so I was surprised and relieved to see them throw the car in reverse and start heading out of the parking lot.

Unfortunately, this was also about the exact moment that I heard sirens pulling into the complex. Instead, of dropping my weapon and surrendering, I immediately spun around and bolted up the stairs. Each building in the complex had eight apartments—four upstairs and four downstairs, with storage units in the middle of each building. Before re-entering my apartment, I opened the door to our storage unit, and placed the pistol on the door frame, above the door. As I entered, I saw Eddie standing in the living room with my hysterical girlfriend. I instructed Eddie that when the cops come to the door, tell them I'm sleeping and that I haven't been out of the apartment that night. Sounded like a brilliant plan, under the circumstances. I took my girl's hand and quickly led her to my bedroom down the hall. I threw off my clothes, put on a different color tee shirt and jumped under the sheets. To the best of my memory, she was still being defiant, remaining in her clothes, but still climbed into bed. I was hoping that if I closed my eyes as tightly as I could, I would open them and it would be a new day, and this would've just been a bad dream. The police were banging on the door in under two minutes.

`Immediately, I heard Eddie and the police having a loud discussion, as they ordered us out of the bedroom. In what could have been an Academy Award-worthy performance, I slowly shuffled down the hall, "What seems to be the problem, officer?" I uttered, as I yawned and rubbed my eyes. I saw their guns drawn at their sides, but was relieved they weren't pointing at me. *My amazing acting job must be working!* The police immediately began questioning me about a gun and a fight at the bar. I stayed in my Rip Van Winkle character, as I explained to the officers that I had been home for a couple of hours. The officers seemed very skeptical and confused, so they turned to my girlfriend and asked if she had come willingly. In her typical psychotic fashion she replied, "No, but I'll stay." Stunned, I began to argue with her, as the two confused officers looked on. Finally, I think these two rookies had had enough of this white-trash drama, and miraculously decided to get the hell out of there, with only a warning for us. I have had many close calls like that in my lifetime, where desperate times have called for desperate measures. The gift of B.S. and the ability to think like a smooth criminal have helped me get out of a number of scrapes. It was also a huge blessing that the officers of the Panama City Police Department weren't the sharpest tools in the shed.

Exhibit A: A couple of years later, while I was working at Spinnaker, I experienced my first real stalker. I'm talking a real "cuckoo for Cocoa Puffs," bat-shit crazy stalker! This lovely linebacker of a lady was making my life a living hell. I had never even had a conversation with her, until she started telling my coworkers how hot and heavy we were. After some ribbing from the staff, I asked her to stop. Just for the record, you can never reason with a crazy mother effer The more I told her to stay away, the more she kept coming back. Finally, I was forced to ban her from the club. One night as I was driving home I noticed a car following me. She found out where I lived and would show up, sometimes with others, and bang on my windows, demanding I talk to her. One day, I'd had enough, so I grabbed the club's other deejay as witness, and headed straight to the police department. As we walked in, a couple of the detectives recognized me and started ribbing me. "Look who's here," they laughed. "What did you do now Stevie D?" I was surprised that they knew my name, but then again, they had threatened to arrest me almost every weekend for the outrageous bikini contest that I hosted.

As the deejay, Sam, and I sat down at a detective's desk, I began to tell him of my dilemma. He listened and then responded in his good ol' boy accent, "Well, you shouldn't have fucked her!" Stunned, I turned to Sam and pleaded with him to verify my story. Still no sympathy; just more teasing as the detective turned to his colleagues and said, "Hey, Stevie D. fucked some fat chick and now she's stalking him."

I was imagining a scene out of the movie *Misery*-- I awake one morning with this Sasquatch standing over me with a sledge hammer in her hand, saying, "Now you've been a naughty tootie bootie, I'm going to have to keep you here until you fall in love with me." *Crack!* Sledgehammer to the legs!

The detective told me that there was nothing he could do, so I asked if he would at least call the girl and give her a warning. "I don't want this crazy bitch stalking *me*," was his response. His final advice was, "If this nut case comes back onto your property, you should shoot her and drag her into your house. That way, it will look like she was breaking in."

"Should I write this down?," I wondered. "Which order was that? Shoot and drag, or drag and shoot?" Sam the deejay

and I left in disbelief. Luckily, I moved to LA soon thereafter, so I didn't have to take his advice. (Oh, in case the crazy biotch is reading this, I meant to say that I moved to China.)

As my deejay career started to take off, I quit Camelot Music and have never worked for "The Man" since. I had worked a couple of clubs before I got to The Players Club (seriously that was the club's name). It was a cool spot, with three turntables and laser lights— very high-tech at the time. It was a job I almost lost before I ever even started. Just a week before, I was scheduled to begin my new deejay job, my next door neighbor had a party. Have I mentioned that at this point in my life, I had a chip on my shoulder (more like a boulder), and therefore did a lot of reckless shit?

My neighbor, Edward, was a good ol' boy from Alabama who worked at Cox Pools. He would sometimes tell me about his boss's fine sister who was an actress and he wanted to fix me up (turns out it was Courtney Cox). I met her out here in LA and told her about this fascinating little tidbit. She seemed underwhelmed.

Anyways, Edward was having a little soirée (if that's what you can call a bottle of Jack, some Budweiser beers, and cheap weed). I, of course, had lots of alcohol in me and was talking to a girl when she happened to say something like, "This party is boring!"

I replied, in my typical smartass fashion, "Oh, yeah, well watch this!" With that, I ran straight out through the open, sliding-glass window, and jumped off the balcony. Maybe I should get credit for starting Parkour?

Now to say that my stunt went awry would be a huge understatement. As I placed my hands on the balcony railing to launch myself over, I became immediately aware that the railing was not bolted to the balcony! As I was plunging head-first toward the concrete patio below, my only thought was, "This is going to fucking hurt." And it did! I shattered my wrist. I don't know how it works in bigger cities, but when I was brought into the emergency room and was told there was no doctor available, they gave me some serious anesthesia that knocked my ass out. I was awakened around 5:00 a.m. with a killer hangover already setting in, and three nurses holding me down, while the doctor grabbed my arm and began to reset my wrist. Not a pleasant way to start my day.

I had a full cast when I went in to speak to the manager of the Players Club, the day before I was to start working there. I had quit the other club to take this job. I had no savings, credit cards or other means of support. Although the manager was cool, he said he could not risk having a one-armed deejay in this huge club. I assured him I could still do the job, and for the next six weeks, I was the hardest working deejay in Florida!

The Players Club was a year-round club, but I got a call from the owner of a previous place I had worked to come and spin at his new beach club. It would pay double what I was now making, but like most clubs on the beach, it would only be open for the summer. Now, a more responsible person would've stayed at the current job where there was security, but I was definitely not responsible. I took the new job. The place was located way at the other end of the strip where there were no tourists, and it was a disaster. The club closed in only a couple of months. I was out of a job and money, again.

I was basically homeless, sleeping on a friend's couch, when I got a call to come and audition at my dream club, The Spinnaker, the same place that I saw when I visited Panama City in the 11th grade, and had vowed I would come back and be their deejay. I got the job, however, it only paid $50 a night and was just two nights a week. I worked there until the end of the season, and then everything on the beach closed, leaving me jobless and couchless.

I moved over to Tallahassee and crashed with a girlfriend and got a gig spinning at club while I dabbled at the community college. I had some friends there, who were attending Florida State University, with whom I would hang out sometimes, but as with most situations in my social life, I didn't fit in. These guys came from supportive families with structure. They had plans for their lives, but I had no plan, other than to be famous. When spring came, I ended up going back to Panama City and getting my job back at Spinnaker, but this time as the full-time deejay, spinning six nights a week, eight hours a night.

I would come in at 8:00 p.m. and deejay straight through until closing at 4:00 a.m. That's a lot of vinyl-slinging! (Yes, kids, we actually played 12-inch records. Real club deejays still do.) There's nothing like feeling that vinyl on your finger tips as you guide the crowd, building the party energy up until the crowd is ecstatic, or at least wasted enough to dance with uninhibited abandon. At the end of the season, I had an offer to move to Atlanta and live with some wild-ass guys I had met over the summer. I only had a couple hundred dollars and a Fiat convertible that would break down unexpectedly, but still I took off.

When I arrived in Atlanta, I discovered that the guys had just been evicted from their apartment. *Shit, I was homeless yet again!* I called a couple of guys I knew from Panama City and crashed for the winter at their place. I took a job spinning at an all-black club downtown, called Club 131. The owner was a pimp I was always chasing after, for my money. The back of the establishment was a strip club that he also owned. Most of the dancers had stretch marks, bullets wounds, or both. This was a very dangerous part of town. My first night working was awkward, to say the least. I stared out at the packed club as I started to do my thing with no response, only cold stares. A night club deejay usually starts the evening with slower-tempo songs and builds the tempo as the night progresses. You have to pace the crowd and not play all the hits too early in the evening, saving the good shit for later. After about 30 minutes, I started to panic and began breaking out the hits. *Surely this would get them off their asses*, I thought. Still, nothing. *Okay, enough of this shit!* I grabbed some records of much faster BPM (beats per minute, or tempo) like *Push It, Meeting in the Ladies Room* and *Wanna Be Startin' Somethin'*, but I still got nothing but stares! Finally, a guy approached and introduced himself as the deejay of this place a couple nights a week for another promoter. He asked if he could spin a few. *Sure, what the hell.* He was black, by the way.

He immediately dropped the tempo way down and threw on some old school funk, *More Bounce to the Ounce*, and BOOM—there was a tidal wave of dancers! *What the fuck?*

This is honky deejay discrimination! I learned a very valuable lesson that night—brothers don't like to dance to anything over 112 beats per minute! This rule still applies today. Trust me, you will never see a respectable black man dancing to *You Spin Me Right Round*, which is130 BPM.

My final summer season at Spinnaker was complete mayhem. Panama City Beach is famous for its bikini contests, and Spinnaker had a big one on Saturdays. Girls would come from all over the South and enter these contests, hoping that their parents, who paid for their college tuition, would never find out. Fortunately for them, this was before smart phones and Facebook. The club had a piano player named Frankie Golden (I'm pretty sure it was a fake name). This guy would do shots with the crowd and perform party songs all night long like *Mony Mony* and change the lyrics so the drunken crowd could chime in,"Get laid, get fucked!" Brilliant, right? Frankie would also emcee the bikini contest. After being awake all night, he would slam a couple of shots and whatever else needed to get his energy up (snort, snort), and go out in front of the tourists and do his thing. One of my first days back for the summer, Frankie had a fight with the club owners, and quit. They looked at me and said, "Can you handle this?" I said, "Hell, yes," and the rest is Redneck Riviera history!

After my hosting job that day, the owner offered me a new position--entertainment director. I was given the keys to the kingdom! I was just 22 years old. My job as E.D. was to create and host events that would generate more revenue for the club. That was easy—more bikini contests! Oh, and we also did a male strip show for the ladies on Saturdays nights. Ladies got free drinks from 7:00-9:00 during the show, and no men were allowed. The wildest ladies at these shows were always the most conservative by day—bank tellers, teachers, etc.

I hosted seven shows a week. In my mind, this was a great opportunity to hone my hosting skills. *Hi, MTV, this is Stevie D. I hosted 200 bikini contests in Panama City Beach. You've probably heard of me. Why, yes, I am ready to come and be a veejay now.* Actually, I did call MTV, all the time. I even got the president of the network on the phone once and told him to send cameras down, because this place is going off! The year after I moved to California, MTV finally listened to my suggestion, and did just that. I did meet some really interesting and fun people. One of them was Sophia Bowen. She was a celebrity in the Southeast. She was Miss Georgia and had the record for wins on *Star Search* as a spokesmodel (a model who can speak—what a concept). More about her, later.

At the end of end of that crazy season at Spinnaker, I felt I was ready for the big time—L.A. baby! I packed my car with a couple of suitcases, some cash and a framed Elvis movie poster, and hit the road! *Go West, young man, go West!* "But, wait, shouldn't you have a game plan?" my rational voice said to me. Of course, I tuned out this rational voice by cranking up some Van Halen on my cassette player and kept on rolling. I chose Interstate 10, since it's a straight shot from Panama City all the way to Santa Monica, California. Of course, I was way too naïve and cocky to have come out ahead of time and attempt to set myself up in anyway whatsoever. As Bob Seger sang, "I wish I didn't know now, what I didn't know then."

12

The Man with the Golden Hands

I finally have an appointment set with Dr. Williams, the man I've been trying to track down. In addition to being one of Kaiser's leading surgeons in the field of prostate cancer, his bio lists info on his personal interests, which includes coaching baseball for his two sons, and also says he is an advocate for leading a healthy lifestyle following surgery. That's it! I'm all about living a healthy lifestyle before and after surgery, and I also have two little ones who depend on Daddy! *You are my Sensei; I shall be your grasshopper, Dr. Williams?* Oh wait, I told his nurse that this is to be a consultation. I have no idea if Dr. Williams will even consider me for surgery.

While I wait patiently for my appointment with The Man, our family continues to receive prayers from friends, mostly Katie's. Although I've only told a few of my friends, my family knows but we don't receive many well wishes from them. Shit, even though I'm not surprised, it's still very disappointing. My family has never been the affectionate type. I have only one niece and one nephew on my side (who are now adults), and I haven't even heard a word from them. Even though my sisters attempt to defend them, I see daily updates on their Facebook pages, so I know they aren't that fucking busy (making a mental note now regarding my will).

Feb. 8th- Dr. Williams-

After the two-hour drive to the hospital in Riverside, I have to go to the bathroom! Damn, when will my stomach get back to normal? This Kaiser isn't as nice as the one in Irvine, where Dr. Chuang is based, but that's okay. I'm not here to critique the curtains. As I sit in the waiting room, I start to thumb through my folder and all the notes I've taken since this all began. I have names and numbers scribbled all over the place. I glance down at to the bottom of a page and see the words "E-Z Glide!" *Huh? Oh, no! I've been inundated with so much information, I can't keep it all straight! What is "E-Z Glide?" Please don't tell me it's some butt lube? Was this product recommended for one of my procedures?* I start to panic, when I suddenly remember! We have a broken sliding closet door in our bedroom, and this was a number to a closet repair store I was given! (Note to self—pay more attention where I write notes.)

Back to reality, I start to imagine what Dr. Williams' examining room will look like. I'm betting it will look like a king's lair—priceless paintings, bear skin rugs, and medical instruments made of gold! Surprisingly, the room looks like any other examining room—clinical and boring. As I wait nervously while trying to remember my questions, I expect a trumpeter to barge into the door at any minute to announce his entrance: *"All rise for The Man with the Golden Hands, Dr. Stephen Williams!"* Instead, his nurse comes in to take my temp and blood pressure. She tells me that I am so young to have this type of cancer (this comment is starting to sound like a broken record), and she comments on how good my blood pressure is. *"Wow, we don't see this very often, especially with your type of cancer!"* That's because the average age is a thousand! Now where is my Sensai?

I hear a man's voice outside the door. He sounds friendly. He's not barking orders or berating the patient he's speaking to. The door opens and in strolls the man. (Hey, what happened to the trumpeter?) The man is tall, healthy-looking, early 50s, very affable, and relaxed. He smiles, introduces himself, pulls up a stool, and rolls the computer monitor to his side. Impressive! Now this guy must be extremely busy, and even though he knows I already have surgery scheduled with another surgeon, he doesn't seem to be the least bit annoyed or rushed. He looks me in the eye and patiently explains the procedure, and asks if I have any questions. *Yes, a million, but I'll narrow it down to 10 or so.* The first question I ask is how did I get prostate cancer? I keep hearing it's hereditary, but I haven't known of anyone in my family who has had it. However, I do know that an ex-girlfriend had ovarian cancer last year. Could it be related? Shot in the dark, but thought I would ask. He calmly says it's not related. I wonder if these brilliant surgeons ever lose their patience when people like me asks stupid questions. *"Shut up and let me do my job dummy!"* He tells me that there's only about a 10 percent chance that the cause is hereditary. He says more than likely it was caused by something environmental. Environmental? Well, since I don't recall ever wearing asbestos underwear, someone had better get Erin Brockovich on the phone!

Dr. Williams asks if I've seen the DVD. *What DVD?* He seems surprised that no one has bothered to show me the informational DVD about prostate surgery. He cues it up, and leaves the room as I watch. It features four elderly men with prostate cancer, and shows the robotics surgery in action. Hmm, I'm wondering if this DVD has the bonus feature *Where Are They Now*! I want to see video of these old guys five years from now, laughing, bungee-jumping and getting into bar fights.

Dr. Williams returns, and as we start to wrap things up, I still have no idea if, or when, he will do the surgery! I mention Dr. Agus, who had referred me to him, hoping to score some points. Finally, I just come out and ask him the $10 million question, "So would you be able to do this operation?" (Drum roll) He says yes! Cha-ching! Confetti drops from the ceiling, sirens start sounding as I jump off the table and kiss him right on the lips! (That part took place only in my head, of course). Before I can celebrate, I suddenly remember that I already have surgery scheduled with a very competent doctor in Irvine. *Am I allowed to just change surgeons?* Dr. Williams says he will email me a few possible dates.

Now I have a serious decision to make. I feel confident in Dr. Chuang, and he was gracious enough to agree to cut on me, but this is the MAN I've been trying to get and now I've got him! Hmmm…this is a tough one. If I go with Dr. Williams and my surgery is somehow botched, it will be my own fault. Besides, would it be bad karma to change surgeons? What If I die on the operating table and get to Heaven? *"Hey, God, I know I was an ass for some of my life, but you know I cleaned up my act, the last seven or eight years, right?"* But God says, "Yes, you were earning some good points, but you changed surgeons. Bad move, you greedy nincompoop!" Contrary to popular belief, the voice of God did not sound like Morgan Freeman.

Before I even get to my car, I make my decision—Dr. Williams it is! *Damn, I hope this turns out alright!* There's only one problem here—Dr. Chuang and his team are on the schedule. My wife is very organized. I am much more laid-back about things such as where to be and what time we're supposed to be there, and believe it or not, I don't even smoke the ganja! We wait a couple of days until we finally get a message from Dr. Williams. He offers me a date, March 17th. *I'll take it; I'm there, dude!* We try to confirm with his nurse, his surgery coordinator, anyone on his team who will listen. Finally I speak to him again. He says it's on, and that's good enough for me!

Unfortunately, my February network pitches with Tommy Lee are pushed back three weeks because of Tommy's schedule. Damn, I took this gamble because I need to sell *Rockstars of Comedy* ASAP for the security of my family, and now I have to walk around another six weeks with this evil disease that's trying to eat my organs! Shit, is the beginning of the bad karma?

13

City of Angels….and One Hillbilly

After driving for three long days, I finally see the road sign I've imagined a thousand times—"Los Angeles." I didn't get too many kicks on Route 66, but I did have plenty of time to reflect. However, I would say that somewhere around Texas, the fear started to settle in—*What the fuck am I doing?* Oh well, too late to turn back now! Besides, I had nothing to turn back to. Everyone should drive across the United States at least once in their lifetime. My only advice would be to avoid the state of Texas. It's flat and it takes about 15 hours to cross. It's especially eerie at night. You see a lot of signs for state prisons and then another few miles down the road will be a sign that reads "Do Not Pick Up Hitchhikers!" Really, like I'm going to pick up a crazy–eyed dude with a swastika tattoo on his forehead to discuss the philosophies of life?

"Hey, Buddy, where ya heading? I'm on my way to L.A. Why do you have a switchblade? Are you going to clean your nails? Do you have a job interview? Well, good grooming is important, especially when you're starting a new life. What do you mean I have a pretty mouth?"

My plan was to meet up with two other buddies and crash with them until I got my bearings. One of the guys, Chris, was a male stripper from Atlanta that I had met at Spinnaker in Panama City Beach. The other friend, Brian, was a lifeguard in L.A. They came out a month before me to get settled, but before I arrived, Brian was killed in a motorcycle accident. These guys were wide open, always on 11! Chris was on steroids, a state champion wrestler and always looking for a fight. Soon after Brian's death, another guy from Georgia, Mike, came out to take his place. These guys were there to party and I was coming out to become a legend. Actually, Chris thought he would also be the next James Dean, but was more like a "Rebel Without an IQ."

I had a cool setup my final summer in Panama City. I was renting a stylish, furnished condo on the beach. My West Coast digs were a different story. These guys had rented a one-bedroom apartment with no furnishings whatsoever. The three of us were forced to sleep on an air mattress in the living room because the bedroom was full of suitcases and clothes. Within a month, Chris invited another one of his male stripper friends to live with us. Now I'm living with the white trash Chippendale wannabes and we're all sleeping on one air mattress. We had to turn the mattress diagonally, with our feet hanging off the end so we could all fit. The blaring sun would wake us at the crack of dawn because we didn't even have a curtain over the sliding glass door (which was also the only door). By this time, the mattress would be deflated and our feet would be asleep. As if the situation wasn't glamorous enough, soon the toilet was broken, the shower was clogged and our heat was shut off. Lucky for us, the apartment next door was vacant. Before hitting the town, we would go next door and shower with cold water and no electricity. Chris had fortunately brought a few of his male stripper costumes with him, which included a gorilla and Darth Vader. (Apparently women are freaky and enjoy those kinds of things!) These costumes came in handy when one of the roommates would be next door showering. There's nothing like coming out of a cold shower in the dark, after breaking and entering, and Darth Vader jumps out and scares the shit out of you!

Chris' motives were similar to mine and those of thousands of other hopefuls in this town—to be the leader of the pack. A teacher in high school once told me that she believed I would be a politician one day because I have a way of making people follow me. Chris now has his own followers. After enduring the pressures of L.A. for many years, he packed his bags and headed back to Atlanta. He now is a minister and actor, starring in a huge production of *Jesus Christ, Superstar,* as J.C., of course. Preach on brother!

After six months of living in our den of debauchery, I received a call from Sophia. Sophia had lived in L.A. before, and although she enjoyed a lucrative career as a model, she was lonely so she had moved back home. She said that she wanted to come back out, now that I was here, and maybe we could get a place together. Well, it would be really hard to give up the life I had become accustomed to, living with three cavemen, but I'd be willing to give it a shot. Strictly as friends, of course! (Wink, wink.)

Sophia moved out and we got a great place in Hollywood, thanks to her good credit. But wait, every man's fantasy got better—Sophia's successor to the Miss Georgia crown, Donna Rampy, called and was also moving to L.A. and looking for a place. *Come and knock on our door, take a step that is new, where the kisses are hers and hers and his...Three's Company 2!*

The only thing better than one Miss Georgia is two—or maybe seven—but let's not get greedy! I know the men reading this are starting to hear the 70s porn music beginning to play about now, but it didn't go down like that. Sophia would've Lorena Bobbitt-ed me if I had sampled another Georgia peach while she was away on one of her modeling assignments. Oh, by the way, have I mentioned that she and I had started dating? Hmm, funny how that worked out.

Dating a beautiful model in L.A. is not a good idea, at least when you are a struggling artist who is trying to stay focused. Sophia would come home almost on a daily basis with another business card from a "producer" who had approached her, offering to take her to lunch to discuss her career. Hey guys, if you want to meet hot, desperate girls in L.A., stop by Kinko's, spend $40 on some business cards that say "producer," and you're in!

Sophia and I dated for a couple of years, but it eventually fizzled out after she realized, like the others I've dated, the D Man had a plan that did not include marriage for many more moons to come. Or maybe she didn't believe in me as I much as I believed in myself, and had lost faith. After all, she saw me struggle and face rejection a hundred times in those two years. Success came very easily to her.

Example: One day after an audition for some shitty music video, where I would've been a background dancer and gotten paid 50 bucks, I stopped by a tanning salon. (Hey, maybe that's where I got the cancer!) Sophia always knew my schedule, so when I arrived, the receptionist told me that Sophia had called a couple of times, so I called her at home before getting my fake bake. (This was before we had cells phones. The kids are going to think we came from the Stone Age when they read this.) Sophia sounded excited as she explained that she had booked not one, not two, but three national commercials that day!

Now there are several different types of commercials. One is the local commercial, like small businesses such as restaurants, car dealerships, etc. Another type of commercial is the public service announcement (PSA), usually for a nonprofit organization dealing with issues like smoking, bullying, sexually transmitted disease-prevention or the like. The third and most lucrative type of commercial is the national. These are car commercials, sodas, perfumes, etc. An actor in one of these can make $30,000 to $100,000 dollars per.

I tried to sound excited for her. "Hey, that's great! I'm going to stop by El Polo Loco on the way home. Want me to pick you up a burrito? Wait, I only have three bucks on me, how 'bout we spilt one?" This could've been the day that she started packing!

Among my other conquests (girlfriends) was a poor little rich girl, Hathaway, who happened to be from a very prominent American family (the Gambles, as in Proctor and). I met her in a gym in Beverly Hills where I was training her voice teacher. I had also taken a couple lessons from this lady, where she made it clear that she wanted to teach me more than vocal scales. Although she was attractive (she reminded me of Ginger from *Gilligan's Island*), I could tell that she was nuckin futs! I would be sitting on the piano bench next to her and she would place her hand on my knee for encouragement while I would sing. I wasn't sure if this helped the quality of my voice, but if her hand slid higher, I'm sure I would've gone up a couple of octaves. One day while I was working out, the teacher came by the gym and asked to speak to me. She proceeded to tell me how she was aware of my relationship with Hathaway and how she could not allow this to happen! She shared a "secret" with me. Her secret was that she had an imaginary friend named Frank. Frank had brought me into her life and told her that we were meant to be together. I told her that I sincerely believed that Frank was crazier than she was! I luckily never saw the teacher again. Maybe she and Frank are living happily on Gilligan's Island!

As difficult as it is to date a model in this town, it is just as difficult to date a rich girl, because their friends are usually also rich. Hathaway and I would meet her friends at some of the nicest restaurants in town. Rich people do this crazy thing when the check comes that my friends would never do: they split the check evenly, no matter what everyone ordered! There would usually be one guy at the end of the table pretending to be Donald Trump, ordering wine and dishes of expensive food for the whole table, but when the server would give him the check, he would announce, "Hey, the bill is $1200, so if everyone kicks in $200, we're good!"

We're good? Who's good? I had some chicken and a Heineken, here's my $40 bucks! Hathaway would usually kick me under the table and whisper that she's got it! My friends would never try to pull a pretentious move like this when we were out drinking. (Besides, real men don't go to dinner together). We scrutinize every item on the check. "Hey, who ordered the Long Island Tea? That's a $12 drink! We will not leave this bar until somebody kicks in this missing $12!" I would smash a Heineken bottle over someone's head just on the principle! That's how real friends drink together.

Even though Hathaway pretended to be cool with our huge gap in incomes, I could tell we were doomed. After dating a very short time, she informed me that we (she) were invited to her friends' wedding that would take place on a vineyard in beautiful Sonoma, California. She told me that we were going to be staying at the Mission Valley Spa, where she already had us booked for three nights and had paid for our flight. I started to protest until I remembered that this was the friend whose sister was the model Carrie Otis. Also, the fact that Hathaway was picking up the tab made it easier to say yes. This could be a fun shindig! Maybe after a couple of cocktails and other mood enhancers, I could ask Carrie, "So, when you were married to Mickey Rourke, did that gun accidentally go off, or did Mickey shoot you? Enquiring minds want to know." (Mickey and Carrie were allegedly arguing once and somehow her purse fell on the ground and a gun fell out, fired and injured her).

The wedding took place outside of a beautiful farmhouse located on an incredible vineyard. The only landscape that could be more breathtaking would be Tuscany itself.

After the ceremony, the party got started with a cool Cajun Zydeco band. Thinking I needed to get something in my stomach before I got my hillbilly freak on, I grabbed two chicken quarters off the grill and started putting them away. They looked great on the outside, nice grill marks perfectly charred across the skin, but I did notice that the chicken seemed somewhat slimy on the inside. What the hell, I was drinking and laughing and having a good time when someone at the table said something to the effect of, "Hey, that chicken is pink, don't eat it!"

"Don't eat it?," I said. "I've already eaten the other quarter!"

I am color blind, so I couldn't tell if the chicken was pink, purple, or blue. It was free, and that made it taste even better. I panicked for a second, but then decided to down another vodka, thinking that should kill any salmonella. I had never had food poisoning before, so I had no idea what I was in for. About 30 minutes later, as we gathered around the bride and groom to listen to their speeches, I began to feel very unusual. The vineyard started to spin and I began to sweat while my knees felt like they were going to buckle. I whispered to Hathaway that I needed some fresh air. She looked at me like I had lost my marbles, as we were actually standing outside in fresh air at a vineyard. She stayed close to the festivities as I creeped over to some trees to try to get my bearings. The tree I was leaning against seemed to be swaying , so I decided I really needed to leave immediately, if not sooner. I told Hathaway we needed to get out of there, as in right this minute. She was still listening to the speech and not really looking at me until she heard the sense of urgency in my voice. As she turned and saw my condition, she knew I was serious. She quickly went to retrieve our jackets and informed her friend, Nancy, who had ridden with us, that we were leaving. Nancy decided for whatever reason that she would leave, too. (Nancy is Drew Barrymore's producing partner and is now married to Jimmy Fallon).

I had driven from our hotel to the wedding, but I was in no condition to drive now, so I curled up in the passenger seat and prayed that I wouldn't toss my cookies in the car. Once we got back to the hotel, I somehow managed to walk Nancy to her room. I have no idea what I could've said to her other than, "I see dead people." I was starting to hallucinate. After Hathaway undressed me I remember asking her for more blankets, as many as she could find. Then the first wave hit me! My stomach started to gurgle like Jeff Daniels in *Dumb and Dumber*. Hathaway and I had not so much as burped in front of each other, much less shared bathroom experiences, and that's the way I would've preferred to keep it. Unfortunately, Mr. Salmonella had other ideas! I sprang out of bed and made a mad dash to the bathroom, which was only ten feet away. I slammed the door and made it on the pot without a second to spare! The noises that were coming from my body were so disturbing, I wouldn't have blamed her if she had grabbed her stuff and jumped on the plane back to L.A. without me!

As the anal exorcism continued, another strange feeling came over me— I now had to throw up! *No, this cannot be happening. Is that even possible? How can something come out that end when it's already coming out the other end?* Before I could answer that question, here it came, ready or not! I immediately jumped up from the toilet, but as I spun around to throw up, I slammed my head into the metal towel rack. Can someone just please shoot me? Now I was in excruciating pain, and as I started to yell, I began to throw up! Just when it looked like matters couldn't get any worse, the door which was now located two feet behind my ass, flew open and there stood my beautiful girlfriend in shock and horror! She had heard the crash of my head hitting the towel rack and rushed in to see if I had passed out. She may have expected to see me sprawled out the bathroom floor unconscious. Instead, what she saw was something much more disturbing.

I really wouldn't have blamed her if she had never spoken to me again, because I'm sure what her eyes witnessed will be forever seared into her memory.

I spent the rest of the night in chills, watching the MTV Music Awards airing back to back, over and over. I would take

a sip of water every 30 minutes, get up, run to the bathroom, poop, throw up and repeat. So romantic! By the time Hathaway woke up the next morning, I had decided that if I was going to die, I wanted to do it in L.A.—either in my apartment or in the comfort of her high-rise condo (preferably the latter). I somehow managed to get my things in the suitcase, including the one suit that I owned, and, of course, raid the bathroom of all the toiletries.

A boy has to make a living.

It's the white trash in me. I only hope they were Procter & Gamble products.

14

Smack Down

I recently read Adam Corolla's book *In Fifty Years We'll All Be Chicks*, and in it he says something like all men know a cool fight story, and he proceeds to tell one. Even though I had intended for this book to be inspirational, funny and even heartwarming, it's been months since I started this process, so the testosterone that's returning to my body is telling me to share an ass-kicking story. So here's a little ditty for ya...

In L.A. it's entirely possible to meet several people throughout the day who need the shit slapped out of them. One afternoon, shortly after I had moved to the Hollywood area, my girlfriend, Sophia, and I were driving in my little piece of shit Suzuki Samurai to grab lunch on Sunset Boulevard. If you are ever visiting the area and you're driving a manual transmission car, avoid the intersection of La Cienega Boulevard and Sunset Boulevard at all costs. It's about a 60-degree incline, so you will either burn your clutch out or roll into the car behind you while sitting there during high-traffic hours, which are from around 6:00 a.m. until 2:00 a.m. A NASCAR driver would have a problem on this bitch of a block.

As we inched our way up to the top of La Cienega on this typically heavy traffic afternoon, we finally reached Sunset. We had the red light, but there was a break in the eastbound traffic so I began to make a legal right turn. A tour van approached, and seemed to pause as the driver saw me turning right onto Sunset. It's customary to let drivers in, when possible, at this intersection because of the insane incline. As I proceeded with my turn I looked at the driver of the van, held my arm out the window and waved a "thank you." To my surprise, I heard the van's engine accelerate as I quickly turned to see the driver slamming on the brakes inches from my arm.

Of course I begin yelling expletives at the driver and to my surprise, he was yelling them back at me! *Let me get this straight— I gave you a courteous wave for doing the right thing that will take two seconds out of your day, and you're pissed at me?*

I could tell by his accent that he was of Middle Eastern descent. I think the word he was yelling that really gave his ethnicity away was "Icehole!" It went something like this: "You fucking faggot Icehole! You mother of fucker Icehole faggot! You faggot fucker of Icehole faggot!" ...and so on. This guy was going crazy. My immediate reaction was to jump out of my car, punch him in the face, get back in my car and proceed to our planned lunch at our favorite restaurant, The Source. (By the way, The Source was a very peaceful, hippy, all-vegetarian spot.)

I still had a lot of pent-up anger from a fucked childhood at this point, however, so I made the decision that it probably would not be in my best interest to get into a street fight in the middle of traffic on Sunset Boulevard. Apparently the other driver did not get the memo. As he continued to yell obscenities and tailgate me, I noticed the side of his van read "Hollywood Tours" (not the real name, so no lawsuits please). This psycho actually has a job in customer service. "Hey, there's George Clooney's fucking house. I hear he's an Icehole!" At this point my Southern beauty queen girlfriend was also in the heat of the yelling tirade. She was turned around in her seat yelling insults back, as the van was inching closer and the driver was calling her a "bitch Icehole," or something to that effect. No matter how dignified a Southern girl may look, she's one insult away from removing her heels and going Jerry Springer on your ass.

As I quickly changed lanes, so did the van driver, relentless in his quest for blood. When the traffic came to a complete stop, I looked in my rear view mirror to see him jumping out of his van and running toward me. I realized it was "go" time, so I quickly jump out of my car, all the while thinking, "Damn this crazy fucker is probably about to shoot me right here!" He didn't spend any time discussing the traffic laws, as he immediately began to swing and throw some karate kicks. "Wow," I thought for a second, "I may be in trouble," but then I remembered my girlfriend was watching this shit! Never, EVER get your ass kicked in front of your woman! She will lose all respect for you. Even though she may hold you while you're whimpering, curled up in the fetal position, she will be thinking, "Damn, this little bitch can't protect me. I need a real man!" I deflected a couple of punches before I grabbed hold of him, immediately realizing that I was much stronger than this loudmouth psycho. I took his right leg out with my right leg, and, using my hips, I slammed his head into my rear wheel. It made a pretty ring!

We struggled a little, I punched him a couple of times and he ripped my shirt. At this point I thought it was over, so I was going to leave him laying there, and get the hell out of Dodge. Unfortunately, the traffic had only moved a few feet, so as I was attempting to get back into my car, he got up and came back for more. This was beginning to cause quite a scene, as cars full of passengers looked on. It was obvious after I cracked him a couple more times that this wasn't going to end well for him, but he would not shut his fucking mouth. *What karate school teaches this tactic? When you're getting the shit kicked out of you, just keep calling your opponent names? He may be breaking your face, but maybe you will hurt his feelings?*

We were now standing in the middle of Sunset, right in front of the Comedy Store (this is before I started doing standup) as I noticed a Jeep full of guys to my left stopped in traffic and chanting for me to kick his ass. I just wanted to jump in my car at this point and take off, but the guy was now standing in the middle of the street, still challenging me and running his mouth. I don't recall what he said, but I remember glancing over at the guys in the Jeep cheering me on. I stepped forward and threw a right hook that connected to the guy's temple area, and he dropped to his knees. He was dazed as he looked up, and I saw blood coming from his eye (that can't be good), and the guys in the Jeep went nuts, because they knew this fucker deserved it. I really needed to get out of there immediately. As I jumped in my car, I saw the other guy stumble back to the van, and to my disbelief, he started to shout obscenities at me again! For some reason, I opened my car door, and looked back as he shouted something about calling the police. Really? That's how you're going to take your ass-whooping, by being a bitch and calling the police? For some reason (fucked up childhood more than likely) I jumped out of my car, ran right up to him and kicked him square in the balls! I was wearing work boots, which were very fashionable in the early 90s, and highly effective at inflicting pain to the groin area. After ringing his jingle bells, I jumped in the passenger side of my Samurai and instructed Sophia to drive. She took a right turn and we escaped.

I can only imagine the van driver giving a tour on Sunset Boulevard after that day. "On right you will see world famous Comedy Store, and here in middle of street is where I got my balls kicked in for being an Icehole."

15

The Big Day!

March 16th-

Katie and I are at dinner, one of our favorite restaurants in our area. Our sister-in-law, Tina, and Katie's brother, Kevin, are watching our kids, Colin and Faith. My pre-surgery fast will start in 90 minutes. I wonder if I can drink. Screw it— I order a glass of wine. I just won't mention it to the pre-op nurse in the morning. I want a little alone time with Katie before it all goes down. I've gotten her a card, which I give to her after dinner. It says something to the effect of, "Thank you for being an amazing wife and friend, for believing in me, and most importantly, for giving me the greatest joy in my life, our children." I also tell her how to access important documents on our computer, like contracts for production deals, just in case.

Also, I tell her that if she ever remarries, I will haunt her.

March 17th

Okay, this is the big dance. Katie and I are supposed to leave at 6:00 a.m. That gives us two hours to get to Downey, so we should be fine. Of course I am procrastinating, as we just got a new GPS, and this is the day I decide I want to play with it. We're sitting in the car and, it's almost 6:30 and I'm trying to learn to program it. Katie keeps telling me that she wrote down the directions and besides, I've been there before, but that's beside the point. Two facts about men: we never trust a woman with directions, and we love gadgets. Finally, at 7:00 a.m. we head out. We're sitting on the 101 Ventura Freeway and it's a parking lot! Oops, I've only lived here 23 years, so I should expect some morning traffic. What is wrong with me? Am I trying to sabotage the most important day of my life? I'm not sure, maybe it's just fear. All the way down, we're chatting, but not about what I want to talk about. I just keep wondering if Katie will try to comfort me, reassure me, reflect on all of the good times we've had together. I keep forgetting, Katie isn't the mushy type; that would be me. Opposites attract. Although she has become more sentimental since the little ones came along, I also feel like a scared child right now, who could use some TLC.

We arrive at the hospital and drag in enough bags for a week, even though we're only supposed to stay overnight. We find the check- in, and notice that no one else has bags. The nurse tells us we should take the bags back to the car until after surgery and then bring them straight to the room, but Katie refuses. It's a very small room and it's busy, and Katie wants to use the bags to save seats for her family who is coming to wait with her. She looks like a homeless person crashing out at the bus station. We go to the restroom and she wants to look around the hospital. She saw on the hospital's website that there is a meditation room. She and her two sisters have discussed doing yoga in there during my operation. Great— I'm getting filleted and she's doing the tree pose. We find the tiny meditation room. It's not as impressive as the website described. Disappointed, we head back to check in. I'm getting very annoyed that she hasn't gotten emotional. Maybe I'm just being a baby, but I was really hoping for more than a high-five, "Go rock it," from my wife before I go under. We walk back to the waiting room and it's even more crowded. There is a punk-ass gang-banger wannabe with his legs stretched out. I stop and stare, but he's too stupid or oblivious to have the decency to pull his legs back so I can walk by him. I pause and stare like, "Are you fucking serious?" As I make a big, exaggerated step over his legs, he still doesn't notice. Katie goes around the other way, and we meet at our seats. I'm so pissed and stare back at this dick. I tell her what happened and I want to go back and kick his fucking head in. Of course I'm overreacting, but the fact that I was already annoyed doesn't help. I'm thinking, "What will the repercussions be if I go bitch-slap this ass-wipe? Will they cancel my surgery? Will I get arrested?"

"Hey, Katie, how did Stevie's surgery go?"

"Well, he kicked some guy in the face in the waiting area, and got arrested. When Dr. Williams found out, he refused to operate on a psycho, and he canceled his surgery!"

Damn karma! Luckily the nurse calls my name within 60 seconds. Okay, here we go!

They take me to the back and immediately instruct me to get undressed and put on the gown. They start prepping me right away— taking blood, strapping circulating wraps on my legs, and handing me forms to sign. One form is a release of liability because of sterilization. I'm so nervous that my simple brain confuses this with impotence. I hold off on signing that one. Wait, now I'm not going to be able to get it up ever? Is this the old bait-and-switch routine? I had read in some of the brochures that there was a chance of this happening, but those stats were based on 72-year-old men! I'm so nervous, I can't think clearly.

Both of Katie's sisters, Colleen and Erin, come back one at a time to chat. Dr. Williams comes in to see me, and the nurse asks him about the Probable Sterile form. He reminds me that this surgery is also like a vasectomy; we have talked about this, the cryo banks, etc. Oh yeah, I've got my mind stuck on impotence. "Oops, my bad," I say. I sign the release. The doctor still hasn't met Katie, so he leaves and will return to discuss the surgery with her. In the meantime, a man comes in to shave me from my chest down to my mid-thigh. I guess my insurance didn't cover a Brazilian wax! Katie comes back in and so does Dr. Williams. Again, the man is very relaxed and patient, answering all questions and explaining the surgery to us. He reminds me that he will go deeper on the left side, since that's where my biopsy showed the cancer, so he will be closer to the nerves there. Now Katie decides this is the perfect time to ask him about his unique middle name, Guion! She's been obsessed with it ever since she first saw it. He puts it on everything—"Dr. Stephen Guion Williams." Now I'm thinking, "Oh, no, you just insulted the man who will be cutting my junk in an hour." Fortunately, he has a good sense of humor, and he explains the origin of his name. I believe he said it was Scottish, but I was too nervous to accurately recall.

I'm starting to process all the possibilities of the outcome of my surgery. Dr. Williams said he will try to spare the nerves, (which means my ability to get erections in the future), but if the cancer is in the nerves, or if it looks like a probability, he will have to take them! He will also take the lymph nodes to see if the cancer has spread. Now this is the big-ticket item! I don't mind that this will add another 45 minutes to surgery and longer recovery time; it's got to be done. He says he'll see me at 11:30 and reassures Katie that he will come out and talk with her after it's over. I'm glad that Katie has finally been able to meet the man who holds our future in his hands.

Dr. Williams leaves, and I'm sitting there alone with my wife. "In sickness and in health," I say, trying to lighten things up, but I'm still mad that Katie hasn't even told me any of those things that Hallmark cards say. Hell, tell me something corny like, "You complete me." I'll take anything! I don't want to go into surgery mad. I decide to not make a big deal out of it, so I just ask her for a hug. I tell her that's all I've been wanting all morning. We both get teary-eyed as we hug and both say, "I love you." That was just what I wanted, and it hit the spot. Let's do this!

I go into surgery not knowing how my life, long or short, will be different after this day. The anesthesiologist comes in to wheel me into surgery, and he says, "Hey, remember me?" It takes a minute before it comes to me. This is the guy I saw for my pre-op tests in Downey on March, 2nd. All of these faces and names from my many visits to five different Kaiser hospitals are becoming a blur. I remember this guy for one particular reason—he told me I was the most fit patient he'd ever seen. I answered, "Great, let's keep it that way." I'm happy to see a familiar face and take this as a good sign. I tell him, "Yes, I do remember you. Let's rock!"

He wheels me into the surgery room, and immediately there are around eight people bustling around me. I see a big robot machine with several arms. It looks like a sci-fi octopus! I ask, "Is that the beast?" Someone answers, "Yes, that's it!" They move me over to the operating table and in walks the man, Dr. Williams! He looks confidents and cool, and immediately starts giving orders in doctor language. I try to make small talk with him, but things are moving quickly, I want to say something like, "Take your time in there," but people are strapping me down, and getting me ready for blast off! Within a couple of minutes it was night-night time.

* * * *

I wake up groggy and feeling like shit, with one thought going through my brain—PAIN! Before my surgery, I was thinking about how men always wake up after a near-death experience in movies and say something cool. I look up and see Katie, but she's very blurry. I try to focus as I utter, "This is very inconvenient," followed by, "Let's get this show on the road!" Perhaps I should've given more time to my "cool" speech. In addition, right after this I say, "I have a headache and I have to pee."

The nurse informs me that I have catheter, so I can just pee. Sounds magical! However, I feel like it will hurt a lot if I push. What I don't realize is that I can't even feel that I am peeing. My head is killing me! It feels just like the splitting sinus headaches I get that are accompanied by nausea, times 10.

A cool, young, Latino male nurse or orderly (whatever the title is) pushes my rolling bed to my room. He seems like the kind of guy who has turned his life around. He apparently digs the conversation with Katie because he sticks around a few minutes talking about his kids. I try to chime in, but I'm on a heavy morphine drip and I feel like I'm speaking in tongues. I mumble a few words and literally nod off. "Yeah, kids are great! My son and loves Hot Wheelzzzzzzzzzzzzzzz…"

My doctor says he will put in a request for me to have dinner that night. I'm actually in no mood to eat, but we wanted to get something for Katie. We call to place our order and are told that I'm on the "no meal" list. *Oh, well, sorry Katie, hope you brought a protein bar…zzzzzzzzzzzz!*

That night was miserable. The nurses woke me up about every hour to check everything out. I think they just wake you so they will have a witness in case doctor asks if they were doing their job. At about 5:00 a.m., a nurse comes in to ask if I'm ready to take my first walk. "No, but I'm ready to take my first sleep," I say. "Can you check back in a few hours, or few days?" She fakes a laugh and says, "You can do it, come on!" I literally feel like a Mack Truck has run over me, backed up, and did it again. I struggle, but finally manage to get out of bed with her help. She pushes my IV and my catheter tube. About every four feet, the tube falls and she runs over it, almost yanking it out of me. Every time, she stops and gives the same speech about how they should have a hook on the IV stand to hold it, four more feet and ....Oops! Here we go again. I feel like yelling, "Or you could just hold the fucking tube higher!" But that would require a lot more energy that I can muster up. I'm so glad the nurse woke me for this pleasant stroll.

Katie awakens and we spend the next several hours planning my escape. The doctor had said I should get to go home around noon, but now the nurse is saying they may need to keep me because I am draining so much fluid. My doctor isn't available; he's back in Riverside now, so another surgeon comes in to see me. I ask him about the searing pain in my right shoulder."Did the robot-octopus go haywire and rip off my arm, and they had to sew it back on?" The surgeon explains the pain is caused by the air they pumped into me during surgery. He said the air forms pockets under my nerves and has to work its way out. Air? I didn't get the memo that they were going to blow me up like an Oompa-Loompa!

Lunch finally rolls around and there's still no word on if I can go home. I'm still feeling queasy, so I'm afraid to eat anything. Throwing up right now would not be pleasant. In the meantime, Katie has developed a cold. *"Please, Lord, don't let me get it!"* Around 3:00 p.m. the nurse finally confirms that I can go home, although she says they would usually keep a patient who is draining as much fluid as me. (Translation: "It would be much safer for you to stay, but your insurance only covers one night, so good luck!)

Now for my crash course in "How to Become a Nurse in 10 Minutes." She rushes through instructions on how to change my catheter, bandages, and the drain. She explains that the drain will fill with red fluid, so we need to empty it every 3 hours. When Katie asks what the fluid is, she replies, "Oh, just some fluid from around the area that was operated on." Katie says, "Oh, like blood?" The nurse replies, "Yes, blood, but I didn't want to say that and freak you out!" Oh, like it's perfectly normal to have fluorescent red mystery fluid coming out of my body, so long as it's not blood! *"Damn, Katie, come and check this fluid coming out of my side. What is that—Kool-Aid?"*

We arrive back at our place in Tarzana in the late afternoon. Colin runs to the door to greet us, and wants me to pick him up. "Whoa, slow down, little buddy! Remember Da-da has a boo-boo!" I show him a few of the bandages, but I don't want him to see the drainage tube coming out of my side. I believe that would be way too scary for him. Katie and I have been looking for weeks for a book to read to him to help him prepare for this, but we couldn't find one anywhere. I asked the hospital, and the closest thing they had was a book on a mommy having a C-section. I'm pretty sure it would freak him out even more to think Da-Da had a baby! I decide to just stick to "Da-Da's got a boo boo!"

Katie's parents are there, but have to leave in the morning to get back up to their home in Arrowhead, because a big snowfall is coming. We're expecting bad weather down here also. *Uh-oh—this should be interesting.* I'm still feeling very nauseated, so I only take a couple of bites of chicken salad at dinner and lie back on the bed. That night I take a Norco (pain medication) every four hours, but Faith keeps waking up crying, and Katie is sleep-deprived, so she's getting a little bonkers. She brings Faith into our bedroom to swaddle her on our bed (where you roll the baby up like a burrito), but Faith is fighting it loses her pacifier. Katie loses her cool while trying to find it and rips the covers off the bed and ME (and almost my attached drains)! *This is a relaxing environment for my recovery—my first night home and my wife almost kills me.* I feel like I'm in a foxhole on the frontline, explosions and flying shrapnel all around. Katie apologizes and returns to bed after putting Faith back down. I sleep with one eye open the rest of the night, just in case.

Now that Katie's parents have left, I spend the day lounging around, while Colin looks at me suspiciously. Every night it's like *WrestleMania* in our house. I expect him to climb up on the back of the couch at any minute and shout, "Ah-ha, Da-Da, you're mine now," before he launches his body into the air and crashes down on my mid-section! Luckily he takes it easy on me. He will have to wait awhile for his rematch.

The bad weather that was promised, delivers. The rain does come and it comes hard. Our condo is subterranean so it has the potential to flood. I look out the front door and, sure enough, the rain is only inches from coming in, and rising quickly. Katie calls the manager of the property, but the manager doesn't work on Sundays. Here's where my white-trash, thrifty upbringing comes in handy—anything can be fixed with duct tape! If only the Castaways of *Gilligan's Island* would've had duct tape, they could've patched that hole in the S.S. Minnow and been back on their way to Hawaii! Since I can't go outside and clear the drains, I break out the duct tape and triple-tape the seals of the front door! Bingo, it works!

The first few days, I shuffle around our place and feeling very nauseated. Apparently, the pain pills are the cause, so I decide to stop taking them. I choose an appetite over pain. I also can't sleep much. I have a drain coming out of my left side, along with five other incisions across my torso, and the lovely catheter coming out of my penis with the bag hooked onto a chair on the right side of my bed. Katie and I discussed how

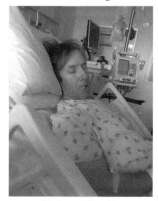

In lots of pain, but still silly.

nice it would be to recover at a relaxing retreat, but I could be at Club Med right now, and still be just as miserable.

I spend a lot of my time the next couple of weeks lying in bed watching *Tom and Jerry* and *Curious George,* with Colin by my side. The one good thing about this recovery is that I get to spend a lot with mi familia. I'm not wired to be idle, so while my body rests, my mind races. I plot my plan of attack on this city. Although, I have pitches

lined up, I start to get ideas for new projects. I have many meetings over the phone, never letting on that I'm recovering from cancer surgery. After what I've been through, this next year should be a breeze. It turns out the breeze is more like a hurricane.

16

Drain, Drain, Go Away!

March 29

The drain number is finally below 100 cc, so it's coming out! I spoke to Dr. Williams last night to get permission to have the drain removed at Kaiser's Woodland Hills location, so I don't have to drive all the way to Riverside again. I call his nurse, but she has no knowledge of this. She says for me to call Woodland Hills, but then she says she'll call first and call me right back, or a nurse from Woodland Hills will call. Or maybe Santa Claus will call—who knows! We talk for 10 minutes in circles. After we hang up I call the Woodland Hills urology department and attempt to set something up. The nurse finally tells me she will send a message there to Dr. BSM! Dr. BSM? Oh, no—he might still feel shunned and this will be his payback! I imagine a menacing doctor rubbing his hands together, laughing and saying, "Ah yes, send him over!"

I wait for hours, but receive no call from Dr. Williams' nurse! Finally, at 2:00 p.m., the phone rings, and it's Dr. BSM! Actually, he's pretty pleasant. He says that I'm at a risk of infection with the tube in me, and asks when I can come over. I say, "Twenty minutes!"

Forty-five minutes after arriving, I begin to think Dr. BSM is making me wait on purpose, but then I hear him outside the room bustling around with other patients. This dude is busy! I start to do breathing exercises in preparation for what's about to come. Finally, he enters, instructs me to pull my pants down and lie back. I inform him that I've had the catheter removed. He says he knows this, so I do as he says. He gets down to business. He begins clipping the stitches and instructs me to hold on, because it will be uncomfortable for a minute. *Uncomfortable?*

He starts to pull on my drain tube and it feels like he's pulling my organs out of my .38 bullet hole! *Yow! The tube must be wrapped around something important!* I immediately feel a lot of discomfort where the prostate was, and the surrounding areas. Dr. BSM tidies up and tells me to see him in his office. The guy doesn't F around! I drop into his office as he types something to Dr. Williams, and I ask him about my weight loss. "Dr. BSM, I've noticed that I have been steadily losing weight the past couple of years. Could this be attributed to the cancer?" Half-listening, he says, "Yes, your body has just been through a serious surgery. This can cause your body to lose weight." *Hmm, that's not the answer to my question, but I decide to quit while I'm ahead.* He answers his phone just as we are about to say goodbye. I guess we are done here. I offer my hand. It lingers mid-air for a few seconds, he notices, shakes quickly, and I'm out the door. Was I supposed to check out with the nurse? Is there other info for me-- maybe instructions for post-drain removal? Who knows, but I'm getting the hell out of Dodge!

I call Katie and tell her to have the kiddos ready, we're taking a big outing to the mall! I stop home to pick up my precious cargo. It now takes about 15 minutes to get from our condo into the car, approximately 40 yards away. Katie carries our little girl, and Colin has to walk, with many distractions during those 40 yards. "Hey Da-Da, look, squirrel, airplane, big rock!" Hey, now he decides to run in the opposite direction for no apparent reason! Da-Da can't run, and Mommy's arms are full. Why didn't I ever learn to lasso? We finally make it to the mall. Colin only wants to go to the mall for one reason and one reason only—cars! There is a Target in the mall, and he can sit in the toy aisle and play for hours. There is also a dealership located in the mall that sells Lamborghinis. Only in L.A.!

After walking about 10 minutes, I start to feel dampness in my crotch area, my balls feel like someone had hit them with a hammer, and my side is soaking wet! My .38 hole is gushing that mysterious bodily fluid! *Hmm...maybe Dr. BSM could've warned me to take it easy, especially since he didn't stitch the hole.* I guess he left it open to heal? Or, maybe for me to get an infection and die? We get home and I have to change the dressing over three times in the two hours before bedtime. I sleep on a towel to absorb the leaking fluid. *For better or for worse, Katie!*

However, all is forgiven with Dr. BSM. I do wish that he could've presented me my news in a different manner, and had gotten me an earlier appointment with him to save myself the daily panic attacks while trying to gather my own information. Maybe he is just a super busy doctor, or maybe he's so used to giving the news of prostate cancer to 72-year-olds. *"Yep, you have prostate cancer, Fred, but hell, you're old anyway, and you've had a good run, so enjoy your next five years of life!"*

17

Rock of Ages

In my years as a comic, deejay and personal trainer, I've had my share of wacky stories involving rock stars. Here are a few you might enjoy.

Def Leppard

One afternoon in September of 2000 I was working out at Crunch Gym in Hollywood, and joking around with a friend, Anita. Anita was a cute biracial girl who happened to be married to Phil Collen, lead guitarist for Def Leppard. I would always tease Anita about getting me tickets to go see the band, which she promised she would the next time they played in Los Angeles. I heard they were in town so, of course, I mentioned it again (because the squeaky wheel gets the grease, or in this case, Def Leppard tickets). To my surprise, she said that indeed the boys were in town but they weren't playing, they were receiving a star on the Rock Walk of Fame on the Sunset Strip. I half jokingly said, "Great, can I go?" She hesitated and then responded, "Uh yeah, I think that would be cool!"

I thought about it after I left the gym, and assumed that after she talked to her husband, I would be un-invited— (In British rock star who-gives-a-fuck accent) *"Who is this bloke Stevie D.? You mean you're telling me on this day when I am going to be recognized for my great achievements in rock-and-fucking roll, I should share this occasion with this wanker? Abso-fucking-lutely not!"*

However, to my surprise, when I called Anita that afternoon, she said it was on and gave me instructions on where to go. Since she didn't think there was any way in hell I could get in alone, she told me to meet her in the parking lot of the Guitar

Center-Hollywood, where the event was taking place. I arrived on time, but was beginning to think that maybe I was being punked. But lo and behold, as I got out my car, I saw Anita waiting there to escort me in. After she showed her I.D. to the security guard, we were both given VIP passes and led inside, and it was about this time that I began to have second thoughts. Yes, this was a cool opportunity, *but what the fuck am I doing here?* This thought was even clearer as I looked around only to find a small number of music execs, and a few females (maybe other wives, girlfriends), more security, and Def Leppard! But definitely no other dude-friends of band members' wives! As Anita began introducing me to the band, I began to really, really have second thoughts. Make that, third thoughts! After a very brief introduction to Phil, I had the strong feeling that the other guys were wondering why in the hell did Phil's wife bring this dude, and I was now wondering the same thing. As if I needed to feel more uncomfortable, I noticed Def Leppard's lead singer Joe Elliott a few feet away from me, talking to a tall man with curly black hair. As I take a second look, I recognize him— it's Brian May of Queen! "Alrighty, maybe I should slip out the back, Jack," I'm thinking; but before I could sneak away, we were approached by a PR man who said, "It's time!"

The PR man, along with some security guys, led us out the front door to the awaiting media and paparazzi. There were camera crews from all over the world on the other side of the velvet rope to capture this moment in history. After a brief speech by some important music exec, Brian May stepped up to a mic to give his props to his mates. As he was giving a great speech about his respect for this band and how they have been mates for many years, I stood there self-consciously. I expected at any minute to be called out by Brian May, "Alright mates, you are fookin' great musicians, you deserve all of your success, I'm very proud to be here, but who the fook is that redneck over there?" I imagined my only response could be, "I'm the new tambourine player, Brian," and with a quick hair flip and a high kick, I would run off down Sunset Boulevard!

After the ceremony, I thanked Anita and said, "Next time, tickets would suffice."

Not Dre's Day

In the early 90s, I was working as the dee jay at a club located in the LAX Marriott at night, and pursing my career in entertainment by day. Five nights a week, I would drive down La Brea through the sketchy Baldwin Hills area, cut over to La Cienega and zig-zag my way over to the hotel. Not exactly living the dream, but it was a pretty fun gig. I was an independent contractor, so I was allowed to do my own thing, to a certain degree. The only complaints I received from management were about the cliental that my music attracted. LAX is located right next to Inglewood, or as Ice Cube pronounces it, "Ingle-Woood!" Apparently, corporate hotel guests are little off put by Crips and Blood. Who knew? It turns out I wasn't the only one to blame.

One evening I walked in to work and discover the club had been rented out for a private party. As I strolled by the bar on the way back to my deejay booth, I noticed some flyers on the tables, so I casually picked one up. The headline read *"O.J. is Innocent."* I immediately got the sense that we were in trouble. A few minutes later, I learned from the management that the party was for rapper, Eazy-E. The manager went on to tell me that the attendees would be people from the world of hip-hop and sports. Guests who were expected included Dr. Dre and Shaquille O'Neal. The manager also informed me that Eazy wanted to bring in his own dee jay, but it was against policy. He went on to ask that I mix the music format up, and keep things under control. In other words, don't play too much rap! At this point I'm thinking that this guy had been dipping into Dr. Dre's chronic. The manager explained that Eazy's record company would also be bringing in additional security, although I soon learned that the additional security was to protect the artists from the hotel security.

Within the first hour of the party, the place smelled like a Bob Marley family reunion. Eazy and the other rappers were openly smoking blunts without a care in the world. Westside! This carefree attitude was not shared by the Marriott staff and management, who were nervously running around, trying to figure out what to do about the situation. On my way back from the bathroom I bumped into Dr. Dre. I had met him once before, so I stopped to say hi, and reacquaint myself. Actually, I was hoping that if someone shouted, "Kill the honky deejay," Dre would step up and and say, "Nah, that white boy is cool, let him slide."

My deejay booth was located in the back corner of the club, right next to the dance floor. You would have to walk through the whole place to get to my booth, right where Eazy and his posse and security had taken over. After a couple hours, things were so crazy that the manager would no longer risk his own safety to get to me to give me more instructions. His brilliant advice up until this point of the evening was to play some nice rock to calm down the situation. Sure, I could see myself jumping on the microphone and announcing, "What's up, party people? Let's hear it for Inglewood! Is Compton in the house? Yea-uh, Yea-uh! Alright, here's some Bob Seger to keep the party going!" And that would be when I would drop to my knees to dodge the bullets.

There was a door right behind my deejay booth that was connected to a restaurant in the hotel. Like an undercover operative, our manager slipped through the door and into my booth. In a frantic voice, he explained that there were many cops outside and instructed me to make an announcement for everyone to leave, immediately; this party was over! I asked, "Let me get this straight, you want me, the only white guy in this room, to get on the microphone and tell all of these hard-core rappers and gang members to get the fuck out? Uh, no, that's not going to work." I told him I had another idea. He wished me luck and snuck out the back door. I reluctantly got on the mic and made an announcement. "Listen up party people, I just got word that the fire department is shutting us down. I know, this is bullshit, but looks like the party is over, the police and the fire department have just arrived. Please exit immediately." After many groans and disapproving shouts of, "Fuck the po-lice," the crowd started to filter out. Shaquille O'Neal was allowed to stay indoors until things settled down. After the club cleared out, I decided to step outside to take a look at things. I had just gotten out in front of the hotel when I heard shots ring out. I didn't care to have a cap popped in my white ass, so I hightailed it back into the club and stayed there for the next two hours. I later found out that the victim of the shots was Dr. Dre, who received two bullets in the leg. Damn, what happened to the California Love? Glad you survived Dre, thanks for being cool to me.

Guitar Gods - The Marriott part II

I was in my deejay booth one evening, spinning some tunes, when one of the waitresses came up to inform me that we had a new manager, and thought we would hit it off. I had never cared to go out of my way to introduce myself to management, so why would I start now? She pointed him out to me. He was about my age, seemed pretty hip, but he was still a suit, and I couldn't be fraternizing with the suits. Later that evening I was on the dance floor, multitasking (throw on a long song and bust a move)! I was tapped on the shoulder, and when I turned around, it was the new manager, Shawn, on the dance floor, too. "Hey, this dude is alright!" I thought. After a few Heinekens and shots after work, Shawn tells me that he just moved from Florida and is temporarily staying in the hotel. He also told me that he plays guitar. Well shit, what are we waiting for, let's rock!

We go up to Shawn's room, where he breaks out his guitar and plays all of my requests full-blast! Hotel guests were calling the front desk: "There are some maniacs in the room next to me playing *Eruption* on the guitar; Can you do something?" Front desk replies, "Oh, we're very sorry, that is one of our managers, we'll have to move you to another room." Shawn and I went on to have many good times over the years.

One evening, Shawn dragged me to see a guitar legend I had never heard of. The player was GRAMMY winner Steve Lukather, who was famous for his work with the band Toto and many other artists. Shawn hailed Steve and Eddie Van Halen as the best players in the world. At the show, Shawn explained that many of the guys in the audience were guitar players, and probably wanted to quit playing after seeing Steve. He was right—the guy was amazing. I also liked his sense of humor. He would play around and even tell dirty jokes between his songs.

Shawn and I would regularly go to a small, nine-hole golf course in Studio City, to embarrass ourselves. We were both horrible but it never bothered us. However, it would frustrate the players who got stuck behind us because we would hold up their game. On busy days, we would be paired up with other players to move things along. This would embarrass Shawn, not because of our lack of skills, but because I would always rent my clubs from the clubhouse. The ones they handed out were the worst clubs on the planet, Sears Cougars, which they striped with orange tape, to ensure you didn't get any ideas about stealing these babies and taking them to the PGA. I would call mine Lady Cougars, because I'm pretty sure they were women's clubs. I would only get three: a nine iron, a seven and a putter. I could've gone to a golf shop and spent a hundred bucks on three cheap clubs, but I thought it was more entertaining to rent these shit sticks, especially since a lot of celebrities would play this course with their expensive, custom-made sets.

I never went to that course without Shawn, until one day when he couldn't make it. I took a neighbor of mine, Victor, who was a riot, only he didn't know it. Victor was a roofer from Dallas, Texas, who had moved to L.A. to become an actor. Victor took more acting classes than anyone I'd ever met, and the poor bastard never booked one job. For one thing, his accent was so damned thick, it sounded fake. He would start every sentence with, "Here's the thang," followed by a story so boring it would make Mother Theresa want to jump off a cliff. I took him to my agency to try to get them to sign him, but after his audition they recommended he go to a voice coach to get rid of his accent. Instead of thanking them for their time, Victor said, "Here's the thang, I don't got no accent." *Ok, J.R., don't call us, we'll call you.*

As Victor and I checked in at the clubhouse, we were told that the course was very busy that day, so they would need to pair us up with two other guys who were just about to tee off. I grabbed my Lady Cougars and headed toward the fairway to meet our victims. As we approached, the guys had their backs turned to us, and one was practicing his swing. I introduced myself, "Hey, guys, looks like we're going to be playing together, I'm Stevie."

The guy closest to me with the longer hair turns and says, "Hi, I'm Ed," just as the other guy steps in and says, "Hi, I'm Steve," as in *Eddie Van Halen and Steve Lukather*. I stand in shock and awe as Victor introduces himself. I warn the guys that I'm fucking horrible, and no matter how bad they are, I will make them look like Arnold Palmer. Eddie fired up a cigarette and we got things under way. I could see that these guys were jealous of my snazzy set of Lady Cougars, so I offered to share, but they declined.

Eddie had a great set of Pings, which he did share with me. I hit a shot that surprisingly landed on the green, so he remarked, "Fuck that, use your own clubs." Steve told me that he had gone to Sammy Davis' estate sell and bought his custom-made clubs, each of which had Sammy's likeness on it, and "The Candyman" written on the bag. Must be nice to be a rock star. I couldn't even afford one of Sammy's spare glass eyes.

I had read that Eddie had just gotten out of rehab, but that didn't stop him from opening a beer and firing up another cigarette at almost every hole. Since then, Eddie has had cancer of the mouth, but in true rock star form, denies it had anything to do with cigarettes, blaming it on the guitar picks that he holds in mouth. I must say that Steve was definitely the nicer of the two. Eddie was cynical, but it was still a very cool experience to get to play with those two guitar heroes. At the end of our round, I told them about Shawn and even got them to sign our score card for him. When I saw Shawn the next day, I handed the card to him and told him that these two guys said to say hi, and to keep practicing. He just stared at it confused, read and reread the names, Eddie and Steve. When I told him the last names were Van Halen and Lukather, he couldn't believe it! We had to call Victor to validate my story. Victor concurred that it was true and launched into a "Here's the thang" story, before I hung up on him. Poor Shawn, he's probably still camped out at Studio City Golf and Tennis Club waiting for those guys to show up again.

Thanks to Meet You

People always want to know what celebrities I've trained. Part of the job of being a personal trainer is to build a repartee with them. Two of my clients that I built a friendship with were John Taylor of Duran Duran and his wife Gela. Gela was the co-founder of Juicy Couture, so I got amazing hook-ups on clothes. One of the best perks of the job was when Juicy would have a private sample sale, and Gela would give Katie and me invitations. With one trip to a Juicy sample sale, we could score thousands of dollars worth of clothes for about $100 dollars. One day when I came in from a training session, Katie was in the kitchen cutting some vegetables with a very large knife, and I casually passed through and mentioned that Gela had given us sample sale invitations. I immediately heard a scream and found her holding her hand, which was covered in blood. In her excitement, she had sliced her finger to the bone, which required many stitches. (Note to men: Never mention a sale when your lady has a sharp object in her hand.)

John and the band were getting back together and for a big reunion tour and invited Katie and me to watch them play at a private show at the Roxy, a very famous rock club located on the Sunset Strip. I was never a Duran Duran fan in high school, but Katie was a fanatic in her youth. I believe the term is "Duranie!"

After the show, we were invited to the private after-party at Chateau Marmont (the hotel were John Belushi died). Katie couldn't believe she was going to get to meet her grammar school crush. Since I had been training John for several years, she'd heard so much about him, but this was their first introduction. As we arrived at the star-studded party, I couldn't wait to find John and introduce Katie. After hitting the bar (first things first), I spotted John deep in conversation with Gwen Stefani and her husband, Gavin Rossdale. A person with better etiquette may have waited until the conversation was over to get John's attention, but I'm from Kentucky and can't even spell that word (thank you, Spell Check), so I blurted right in, "Hey, John, I want you to meet Katie!" Gwen and Gavin looked a little shocked, but John looked really happy to see me and walked over to us.

I had just helped him lose some weight and get his lazy rock star ass in shape, so maybe it was like a proud parent moment. Regardless, John gave me a big hug and I introduced Katie. She attempted to make some sense, but I could tell she was nervous. After chatting for few minutes, we were parting ways when Katie looked at John and blurted out "Thanks to meet you!" John and I looked at each other perplexed, but without a word spoken, he smiled and walked away.

Vegas

Katie and I had been on many weekend excursions, but this was going to be our first trip together to Sin City—Las Vegas. As a single man, I had jaunted over many times. I had even flown over at 4:00 a.m. once, only to sober up after landing, so I turned around and flew right back home. Here's the back story of that drunken night…

I have a crazy, hell-raisin' friend, Jeff, who moved out here from Georgia shortly after I did. Jeff and I were always causing mayhem and competing to out-party the other. After a night of clubbing, we ended up in Beverly Hills at my then- girlfriend's apartment. (I later got her evicted from this apartment, for lighting an M-80 firecracker in the corridor. Oops!) This girl's grandfather supposedly invented the barcode. I never bothered to validate this information, but I do know that we had an open expense account wherever we went. This girl also had a piece of paper that she carried in her purse that read, "I'm sorry for any damages that my daughter may have caused. I will gladly reimburse you for such damages. Sorry for any inconveniences."

As the evening started to wind down, I filled up two glasses full of vodka and challenged Jeff. His girlfriend, Veronica, already had her jacket on to leave, so she obviously thought further drinking was a horrible idea. However, Jeff couldn't pass up a challenge, so we both chugged the full glasses of straight vodka. Jeff is a big dude, 6'3", well over 200 pounds, and very capable of holding an enormous amount of alcohol. Veronica later informed us that Jeff passed out in the elevator and she was forced to drag him to the car. Around 10:00 the next morning, Jeff called me to recap the evening. He asked if we had just gotten up. I said, "No, we just got in—from Vegas!" *I think I won that round, buddy!*

Back to the other Vegas story— On this occasion, Katie and I had been invited by John Taylor to watch Duran Duran play a huge comeback show at the Hard Rock Hotel & Casino. The band was playing for two nights, but we wanted to go a night before to have our own private party. What happened next almost caused Katie and me to adopt. While we were walking around the hotel where we were staying, the Monte Carlo, we noticed a photo booth in an arcade. This particular photo booth caught our interest because it would print a picture of what a child would look like if we were to have one together. Since we didn't have kids yet, we were very curious. How it works is you each go into the booth alone, a computer takes your picture, measures the distance between your eyes, ears, etc., puts your data into the system and, voilà—your baby is born. Or, at least, developed!

Katie and I each went into the booth, and then nervously paced around the arcade. What would our dream baby look like? What color hair would it have? Would it have my blue eyes or hazel, like hers? *Doo dee doo doo, doo dee do…* Anticipation was building! Finally, after about five minutes, our strip of pictures slipped out of the slot of the booth. We both rushed over and snatched it up. On the strip were three pictures—one of me, one of Katie and one of our… wait, *What is that?* We expected to see our beautiful, healthy baby, but what we got was what looked like an 11-year-old hermaphrodite! She had a frilly, *Little House on the Prairie* dress on, and Shirley Temple ringlets in her poop-colored hair. *What the F? This must be a cruel joke!* Surely this contraption could not be anywhere near accurate! After staring at the picture in disbelief, I glanced up and noticed "it" staring at us! There is a picture at the top of the booth of the last couple's love-child displayed, which happened to ours, and it was *winking*, as if taunting us! *"Still want to have children?"* (Wink, wink)

I was outraged, stunned and perplexed, so I immediately approached the manager of the arcade with my concerns. "Excuse me sir," (he was about 18 years old), "we just spent five dollars on what I believed was a very scientific procedure, but I see that this thing really can't be anywhere near accurate, correct? Please tell me that it's just an illusion, like the tigers pretending to growl at Siegfried and Roy." *Oh wait, one ate Siegfreid. Or was that Roy?* The young manager tells me that the magical photo has been very accurate. He tells us that a couple had been in the booth just before us, and that their picture looked *exactly* like one of their three children they had with them. Uh, oh, damn you, weird science! Luckily, neither of our kids was born looking like an 11-year-old hermaphrodite, but even if they had, we would still love them anyway.

Following my afternoon with Katie, I called John and he gave me instructions on where to meet him at the show, and even invited us to the after-party at Simon's. "An after- party in lead singer Simon LeBons' room? This is going to sweet!" Katie and I thought! I just imagined celebrities doing blow off of his coffee table and topless supermodels dancing around. A rock and roll freak show!

The concert was packed! Fans had camped out and a lot of celebrities had flown from L.A. Katie and I were in the back. I was playing it cool. I couldn't be seen dancing in the front row and singing "Wild Boys" at the top of my lungs. But how was I going to get to John? He didn't give me specific instructions on how or where to meet up afterwards. *Shit, I've got to get to Simon's party, but I can't go without John, I'll look like a groupie.* I waited until about an hour after the show before I called John. He was in his room with his wife Gela, freshening up. John instructed me to meet him at the party, but I told him that I wasn't comfortable going without him. He must've been thinking, "What, you can't walk into a party without me holding your hand? What a wanker!" But he hesitantly said, "Okay, Mate, I guess you and Katie can come up to my room and wait here while we get ready." I heard Gela in the background shout, "They can't come up here, I just got out of the shower!" *Hmmm...awkward!*

At this point, I was starting to feel like his little bitch, but John had a solution. Hey, man, just go to Simon's and wait for me at the door, and I will walk in with you. "Okay," I said, "but I don't know where it is."

John replied, "You'll find me." As I hung up, I was thinking, "How in the hell am I going to find Simon LeBon's room?" It's not like I can just walk up to the front desk and ask. "Yeah can you give me Simon Lebon's room number? I hear there's going to be a lot of sex, drugs and celebrities there, and we're ready to party!" As Katie and I were wandering around trying to think of a way to break this rock code, I saw a friend from L.A. who seemed to be in a big hurry.

"Hey, Stevie, what's up, man, are you going to the after-party?"

"Hell, yeah, but what is his room number?"

"Whose room number?" he asks.

"Simon Lebon's," I say.

"How should I know? But the after-party is at Simon's Steak House!"

Huh? Apparently there is a steak house located in the Hard Rock Hotel called Simon's! *Well, shit, Scooby Doo, now the mystery is solved! I didn't get the memo on that one!* I contemplated calling John again, but I would only be digging the "bitch" hole I was in even deeper. We arrived at Simon's to find a lot of paparazzi and a table for guests to check in. In my excitement, I immediately checked in, and Katie I and entered the party and hit the bar! *Hmm... Seems like I'm forgetting something. Oh, yeah, John Taylor is going to meet me out front! Oh, well, we'll just grab a drink and then step out back and check out the party. Besides, I'm sure the lady at the check-in table will tell him that I've already entered.* I was wrong, about 45 minutes later, as I'm standing at the bar singing a duet with Macy Gray to Sheila E.'s *Glamorous Life*, I see John approaching me. "Hey, mate, where were you," he asks, "I've been waiting for you outside." *"Outside? Why would you do that? I'm a big boy. I don't need you to hold my hand! Besides, Katie insisted on coming right in!"* Somebody had to get thrown under the bus!

To say the party was fun would be an understatement. It was epic. I saw celebs and a certain member of the band doing things that I will take to my grave. I don't need Duranies putting a hit out on me!

When I opened my eyes the next morning, I felt like someone had hit me right in the middle of my forehead with an ax! I barely managed to drag myself out of bed as Katie and I threw our stuff into our suitcase and lumbered out to grab a taxi to the airport. We didn't even bother to check out; we just threw our key in the express box. No matter how tired you are, when you step into a casino in Vegas, you will immediately get a surge of energy like you've had three Redbulls. The hotels keep the temperature at around 60 degrees, and it's even been rumored that they pump oxygen into the casinos. I think it's more like nitrous oxide! However the second you step outside, you are immediately reminded you're in the middle of the sweltering dessert. It was 10:00 a.m. and already 100 degrees as we stood in the long line for a taxi. I thought I would literally pass out, but kept telling myself that if I can only make it to the airport, I will be fine. *Well, not fine, but I would be able to throw up in a private area, hopefully!*

When we finally got into a cab, I could not even open my eyes, I just mumbled, "The airport, please?" Of course the driver didn't have the air conditioning on, so I was feeling more nauseated by the minute. As we exited the cab, I threw the driver some money and told him to get his air conditioning fixed. He smiled as if to say, "It works, I was just fucking with you." I was holding on to Katie as she led me to the ticket line. She kept saying she needed to sit down, and I kept repeating that I was about to throw up.

"I need to sit down."

"Well, I need to throw up."

"I really need to sit down."

"Well, if you sit down, I'm going to throw up on you!"

Finally, we made it to the ticket counter. The agent who took our tickets seemed extra peppy as she smiled and asked, "How was your stay in Vegas? Were you lucky?" *SHE was going to be lucky if I didn't toss my cookies on her.*

After handing our tickets back to us, she stared at the screen with a perplexed look on her face and asked to see our tickets again. I peered at her with one eye and handed her our tickets again, while Katie continued to mumble about her need to sit. The lady then informed us in her cheery, animated voice, "I'm sorry but you are here very early for your flight"

"Excuse me, what do you mean? I booked our flights for 12:00, and it's 10:45."

She replied, "You booked your flight for 12:00 a.m., not 12:00 p.m.!"

NO!!!!!!! Okay, I was really, really trying not to hurl, but the airport started to spin. I begged the lady, "Ok, can we just jump on the next flight, or the one after that?" She informed us that all flights were booked, just as they are every Sunday in Vegas.

Katie's solution was to go and sit somewhere for 12 hours. Chair, floor, toilet—I don't think she cared, she just really needed to sit! My solution was to do an about-face, jump right back into a taxi and head straight back to our hotel, which we did. As we stood in the check-in line, I noticed something that I had not paid any attention to before: there were no fucking chairs in the lobby of our hotel! I turned to look at Katie and she was literally sitting in the middle of the lobby with tourists standing all around her.

I calmly, but eagerly informed the check-in person that we had just checked out, I had dropped my key in the express box, and I want it back. No room service—don't even come near the room—just give

Our hermaphrodite computer child.

me my key back ,at any cost! Katie and I returned to our room, closed the drapes, cranked the air to 20 below and slept until 4 p.m. We then woke, went to dinner at Nine Fine Irishmen, and in the spirit of her ancestors, drank a pint of Guinness. We jumped on our scheduled flight without me hurling on anyone.

Hell, yeah! Vegas, Baby!

18

Funny Biz

I didn't grow up dreaming of becoming a stand-up comedian, but I was fascinated with variety television. I saw all of those shows in the 70s—*Sonny & Cher, Donny and Marie, Flip Wilson,* even *American Bandstand*, and thought, "I can do that!" I just needed to find one of those long, ridiculous-looking, skinny microphones like Dick Clark had!

Originally, I came to Los Angeles thinking, "Hey, I'm an amazing, multi-talented performer. This town is going to freak over me!" I guess growing up with very little supervision and a wild imagination can perpetuate delusions of grandeur. However, I realized after about five hours of being here that I was actually going to have to find a way to showcase all of these amazing talents of mine. Pete Townsend of The Who once said that he always knew he was a prodigy; he was only pissed that people wouldn't listen when he told them, so he had to go out and prove it. I felt (and still feel) the same way. After a few years of pounding the pavement, it finally came to me: standup comedy!

First order of business –cut off the mullet. Now I just needed some material. *OK, I cut my hair and now I look like that chick, China Phillips, of the group Wilson Phillips.* There's my opening, now what else could I talk about? Hmm…MC Hammer's career was fading so I came up with some hacky premise like, "What if Hammer did an Ex-Lax commercial and did that silly dance while singing, "Uh oh, uh oh, where da bathroom?' (sung to the melody of *Here Comes the Hammer*?"

My set also included material about growing up poor, and other musical material—Michael Jackson, Elvis, Axl Rose, etc. Really high-brow stuff.

I had heard that The Improv in Santa Monica had a weekly open-mic night. *OK, sounds good, that's a famous place. I'll just start at the top and skip the "paying my dues" in shitty coffee houses, dive bars, and any other hole-in-the-wall that has open-mic nights as free entertainment, not to mention the gay casting couches.*

Which reminds me of an audition I once had to be an MTV host...

I was nervous because this would be a dream job. The job was basically what I had done in Florida, only on television and with a few million extra people watching me (also without the wet t-shirts). I went into the audition and read through my lines once. I felt a little stiff on the first take, and apparently so did the casting director (rim shot here)! He suggested I unbutton my shirt and do another take. *Uh, OK, awkward... but what the hell*, so I did as instructed. After the second take he suggested I take my shirt completely off. I didn't feel comfortable at all, but this guy was the professional, so I took my shirt off and did another take. What a douche bag! This was years before comedian Mike "The Situation" Sorrentino made millions at being a tool.

Needless to say, I didn't get the MTV gig, and never had another audition for them. I believe the guy just used the tape for his private collection. I'm sure casting directors in this town make "best of" compilations and show them at parties. Hell, I even had to pretend to be a spark plug once and jump up and down and make sputtering sounds along with three other grown men. I read that Brad Pitt once had a job standing on the street dressed as the Pioneer Chicken. At least now he's clucking all the way to the bank.

OK, so back to "Improv" story. I rounded up around 25 friends, which included associates and slutty girls, to come and witness this historical event. After slamming a few vodka-cranberries, I made my way to Santa Monica and entered the club. I was instructed to sign my name, and then sit and wait until I was called onto the stage. *Wait, don't I get a long, and much-deserved introduction? What about my theme music and my go-go dancers?* I was truly a legend in my own mind.

In the stand-up comedy world, there is the universal "red light." This is the light that's usually located on the back wall of the club that means your set is done when lit; wrap it up! Unfortunately, this was my first time, and I didn't get the memo on this magical red light. If a comic gets the light, but ignores it and continues with his set, that's called running the light, which is a huge no-no. It could possibly even get you banned from the club (spoiler alert).

I had many questions, including, "How long do I have on stage?" and "What number am I going up?" but the other comics weren't volunteering any information. A lot of comics are insecure pricks that want the other comics to fail miserably, kind of like I did. After sitting through many comics, I noticed they were getting the light at around three minutes. *Well, obviously... because they all sucked!* In actuality, there were probably some great comics on that night, but I had to convince myself that they were terrible to boost my ego and confidence. Finally my name was called. "Please welcome to the stage, Stevie D.," the emcee said in his underwhelmed voice. (BTW, most employees at comedy clubs, besides the waitresses, are wannabe comics who are only working there to get stage time for themselves.)

There was no theme song or go-go dancers, but it was time to rock! I confidently strode onto the stage and grabbed the mic. Note: By this time, I was also pretty pumped from the gym, and as usual for me at the time, I wore a sleeveless vest. Now if there's one thing a comedy audience doesn't want to see, besides a pretty girl talking about how she was an ugly dork in high school that couldn't get a date, it's a guy that is in shape and showing it off. I opened up with a few bits that did not get the reaction I had imagined when I was practicing my routine in the mirror. *Damn, these fuckers are going to make me work.* I dropped the China Phillips impression on them and got a laugh. I was in the middle of another killer, when the emcee interrupted to inform me that the light was on. I could not believe this punk-ass just stepped right on my joke! I told him, "I got it," and continued. About 30 seconds later, he did it again. This time I said "Look, I'm just warming up, Dude."

"No, wrap it up," he said.

I replied, "Why don't we let the audience decide," I asked the audience, "Do you want more?"

"YES!" they answered.

The emcee said, "If you do one more joke, you're never coming back to this club."

I said, "Look, if you interrupt me again, I'm going to kick your fucking teeth in." At this point the energy in the room changed. (Another page out of the *Comedy 101* book— if there is tension on the stage, there is tension in the audience). I started to go into another bit as he talked over me and started the music. *Ah-ha, so they CAN play music! I wonder if next week they will play my theme song, when I return!*

As I said thank you and exited the stage, I confronted the bitter emcee as a couple of my friends intercepted me. I decided to leave, so I made my rounds saying goodbye to my friends as the next comic was trying to get a few jokes out over the disruption. I apologize to whoever this unfortunate comic was. He probably was someone who went on to have a much more lucrative career than I did. As I was leaving, I got into a confrontation with another employee and threatened him, also. I wasn't making many friends in the comedy world so far.

Ironically, this particular Improv mysteriously burned down very shortly after this lovely evening. Now I'm not saying I did it, but I'd like to think that the comedy gods cast down their wrath of anger upon this establishment over my injustice. I had a lot to learn about the L.A. comedy scene.

I decided early on that I would know I had made it in comedy, or at least made it to the big leagues, if I could get my name on the marquee of the world famous Laugh Factory on the Sunset Strip in Hollywood. Now, I pass this marquee almost daily, as do thousands of other L.A. locals and tourists, and there are only a handful of comics that can get their names on that sign. I figured if I could just get my name up there, that would at least get me some of the credibility and the recognition I deserved. In other words, my own bitch-slap to the naysayers who doubted my greatness.

I never intended for this book to turn into my version of Anthony Bourdain's *No Reservations* of the comedy world (great book, by the way), but I will offer a few nuggets from my experiences in this dysfunctional world.

Here's a good story...

After years of playing comedy clubs, dives and whore houses (not really, but a strip club or two), I became a regular at the Laugh Factory and finally started getting my name on the marquee! *"How you like me now bi-atches?"* I would think, every time I saw it. The club's owner, Jamie Masada (who almost every comic can do an impression of) says, "Hey, buddy, listen to me," in his thick Israeli-effeminate accent. "Why you always talk about Michael Jackson and grab your dick on stage?" *Uh, because I enjoy it and people laugh, Jamie.* "Buddy, listen to me, you don't need people to laugh; fuck them." *Well, Jamie, I need "fuck you" money before I can stop giving a fuck what the audience thinks.* Anyway, Jamie liked me, even though he offered to manage me and I turned him down. He said I would need to wear a suit and work clean, be more like Jay Mohr.

I said, "Jamie, first of all, you've seen my act. I'm a hillbilly. I don't even own a suit. And, secondly, Jay doesn't work clean; he talks about how he likes his wife's finger in his ass!" (BTW, he also has "fuck you: money!)

I had a regular show every Thursday night at the Laugh Factory, and it was the hottest show in town. All of the big comics wanted to do my show because it was always rockin'! Regulars included Lisa Lampanelli, Chelsea Handler, Damon Wayons, Dane Cook and many more recognizable funny people from TV and film, and some hot new ones breaking in. In February of 2005, I was at the club doing a spot early in the week, when Jamie called me over and informed me that we would be having a special guest on Thursday, and not to tell anyone. He said he had received a call from the producers of *60 Minutes*. They were doing a story on a famous comic and wanted to come in and film him. They asked what would be a good night, and Jamie told them Thursday—my night. The comic they were talking about was Chris Rock. He was going to be hosting the Oscars and wanted to work out some of his material. Fucking Chris Rock? *60 Minutes*? The Oscars? It's on! Wait did he say not to tell anyone? Well, it couldn't hurt if I told one or two…hundred people! Did I mention that I had a huge mailing list? So Thursday arrived and hundreds of people are lined around the corner and up the street, clammering to get in!

When the *60 Minutes* crew showed up, they could hardly get in the door. *What the F?* They started asking if someone had leaked that Chris was coming. I told them, "Hell, no, these are my fans!" They were afraid that someone would tape part of the show and the secret Oscar material would get out. Dane Cook, who did my show regularly, got wind of things and showed up to perform. Dane went on right before Chris and was only supposed to do 10-15 minutes, but of course he tried to cock-block Chris and take advantage of his audience, and did and hour.

Chris had arrived and was waiting in the lobby while the *60 Minutes* people were starting to get restless. I went in to talk to Chris, and asked him what he would like as an introduction. He said he didn't need an introduction, to just bring him up. *Just bring him up?* No way! I'm thinking, *why would I just bring him up when this is going to be on 60 Minutes? I need to think of a memorable introduction and take as much time up there as possible.* Finally Dane got off the stage after running the red light for 30 minutes.

I sprung to the stage and started the build-up. "Uh, ladies and gentlemen, apparently you were under the impression that a huge comedic star was going to be here tonight. Sorry to inform you that that was a rumor." The crowd knows that I'm f-ing with them and we start to banter back and forth. I'm killing more time up there as I notice all the cameras and see myself on the monitor. *Damn, I look good on TV. I need to kill more time up here!* "Actually, ladies and gentlemen, because of the enormous crowd tonight, we are going to have two shows. This person will actually be on the next show! Please finish your drinks and quickly exit to the left!" After almost causing a riot, I start the build-up for my intro (the one he didn't want). Roll the cameras, *60 Minutes*! I don't recall exactly what I said, except the last part, the sound bite—"Please welcome the VOICE OF OUR GENERATION......CHRIS ROCK!"

OK, a little corny, but hey, I wanted to make an impact! As Chris hit the stage, I gave him the longest handshake in comedy history! The roar from the crowd had almost died down before I finally released my G.I. Joe kung fu grip from his hand! Chris was probably thinking, *"Security, please get this crazy hillbilly off of me!"* Anyway, it was "mission accomplished!" That Sunday night, there I was on *60 Minutes*, bringing Chris Rock onto the stage for his secret show at the Laugh Factory! It was the least I could do, especially for the "Voice of our Generation."

19

For Those About to Roc

*"Don't need no guitar, don't need no band, I rock the stage
with just this mic in my hand."*
—lyrics from *Rockstars of Comedy* theme song

When I was in high school, I would sign my friends' year
books, "I promise not to forget you when I'm a famous rock
star!" When I'm doing stand-up comedy, I always hit the stage
like I'm performing at Madison Square Garden. Whether there
are 40 people in the audience or 400, I'm bringing it! My show
at The Laugh Factory wasn't your typical comedy show. I only
wanted comics up that were hip, edgy, cool, and possessing
the swagger of a rock star. I kept the pace of the show moving
quickly with the way I hosted, and inspiration from my deejay, a
girl named Sketch, whom I brought with me. I realized that with
the Internet, smartphones and 500 plus channels on television
these days, people have a shorter attention span when it comes
to comedy shows than they had it in the past. My main rule for
the comics in my show: "No fucking whining!"

I looked around and saw other comedy tours and franchises
that were hugely successful by catering to certain markets:
Blue Collar Comedy Tour, *Kings of Comedy*, *Latin Kings of
Comedy*, etc., but I didn't see one that catered to my crowd—
the heathens, the hooligans, the fans of whiskey and rock.
I decided to create one, but the name had to be catchy, cool
and dangerous-sounding. And then, it came to me one night
in a dream (or was it six vodka-tonics at Skybar?)—I don't
remember which, but I had it—*Rockstars of Comedy*!

I wanted *Rockstars of Comedy* to have the look and feel of
one of those concert videos from the 80s, except with comedy

rockin' the stage instead of music. I always loved Bon Jovi's *You Give Love a Bad Name* video, especially because it has that shot sweeping over the crowd. I had to have it, and I got it!

The band AC/DC has had a profound, lasting effect on me. I've always loved their raw, blues-driven riffs, their catchy hooks with undertones of naughtiness, and especially their attitude. They don't take themselves too seriously, even when they are laying down some serious rock. My pre-show ritual has always been in my bedroom: headphones on, and a Heineken in one hand, while writing notes for my set. My music selections have always included some AC/DC.

It all began when I saw them perform live on the *Back in Black Tour* as a young, impressionable 14-year-old. Since then, I've had some amazing experiences going to concerts, but nothing can come close to that magical night. Standing in front of the stage at this sold-out, general admission concert was thrilling and terrifying at the same time. The minute the doors opened, it was pandemonium, with thousands of people rushing to get to the front of the stage. Somehow, that's where I ended up. With those thousands of bodies pressing against my small 5 foot, 110 pound frame, it was all I could do to stay conscious and upright. As the lights dimmed, the spotlight shined on an enormous bell being lowered to the stage as the intro to *Hell's Bells* began. The sound of those haunting bells resonated over the crowd as the spotlight hit lead guitarist Angus Young taking the stage like a possessed rock-god Munchkin. Chills ran up the back of my spine and suddenly my fear of being crushed was overcome with exhilaration. I was bulletproof and ready to rock.

Another vivid memory I have of that evening is of someone tugging on my leg. I looked down and saw another one of my friends of ill repute, Mikey E. (real name not disclosed to protect the guilty). He was on his hands and knees, without a shirt, which was not unusual, and shouting something that I couldn't make out over the 100,000 watts of bone-rattling rock. He pops his body up for a minute so I could hear him more clearly as he proceeds to shout, "Hey, man, kick-ass concert, huh? Shit, man, I just stabbed some fucker, so I'll catch ya later!"

His demeanor wasn't what you would expect from someone who had just assaulted another person with a deadly weapon. He had his usual smile, and seemed to be otherwise enjoying himself. In disbelief, I asked, "You did what?"

"Yeah, man, some dude kept stepping on my shoes, so I had to cut him!" I didn't know how I was supposed to react. *"Oh, well, that's perfectly understandable, that bastard got what he deserved."* But before I had a chance to reply, Mikey yells, "Alright, dude, I'll see you at school!" And with that, he drops back down on his hands and knees and crawls off through the crowd.

The following week after the concert, I bumped into Mikey at school and as surprised to see that he wasn't in jail. I askd, "Hey, man, did you get the hell out of there, after I saw you?"

Mikey said, "Hell, no, man, I spent 15 dollars on that ticket. I just crawled up into the stands, took my shirt back off, and watched the rest of the show!"

My only question to Mikey was, "How in the hell did you get a ticket for only 15 dollars?" I don't recall seeing any headlines of someone dying from a stab wound at the AC/DC concert, so apparently that dude also lived to tell a memorable story of his *Back in Black* experience.

I became obsessed with every detail of *Rockstars of Comedy*— the logo (which is the same font used by AC/DC), the line-up, the look, the music, the venue, and even the theme song, which came to me one day while driving over Coldwater Canyon in Los Angeles. I started thinking about songs like The Scorpions' *Rock You Like a Hurricane*. I wanted our theme song to be a rock anthem, to make a statement. I pushed the pedal down on the Trans Am and started hugging the tight Canyon curves, and that's when the chorus hit me. I immediately called my buddy Mark Holt in Memphis and expressed my excitement. After I had the lyrics completed, I recorded a scratch demo here in LA and sent it off to Mark. Mark, who is an accomplished musician and singer, took it into Arden Studios along with his band, and crushed it. Mark's dream was to become a rock star himself, but he had to put those dreams aside to provide for his family in the more secure world of advertising. Ironically, one of his children is now a huge Disney star, Olivia Holt. Rock must be in our DNA. I only hope hell-raising is not.

Rockstars of Comedy is much more than a comedy performance; it's about attitude and lifestyle. The comics I picked were all headliners and friends I had worked with, whom I knew could bring the swagger that I wanted— Dan Levy, Bret Ernst, Sam Tripoli, Bryan Callen, Steve Byrne, and Whitney Cummings. Whitney and Steve went on to get their own TV sitcoms. *You're welcome, America.* I also had Adrianne Curry (winner of *America's Next Top Model*) to introduce me just for eye candy. Her intro: "This guy channels 70s rock better than Led Zeppelin....Stevie Fucking D.!" Not too shabby, Adrianne Curry!

The *Rockstars of Comedy* DVD was released to rave reviews.

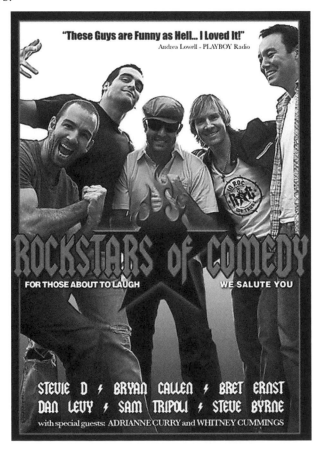

20

The Nutty Nurse

March 24th

Katie and I head to Riverside Kaiser Hospital, where I'm scheduled to have my staples , catheter and drain removed. Riverside is roughly 70 miles away, so I had called the day before with some questions for the nurse before driving all the way down there. My questions included: *Should I take pain meds before the appointment? When am I supposed to take the antibiotic Cipro, because I was only given one when discharged from the hospital? Will my lymph nodes analysis results be ready?* I also had some concerns about my drain; I seemed to still be having a lot of fluid draining. I called Kaiser and was put on hold for the nurse I was scheduled to see. Finally the receptionist came back on to tell me the nurse was on the other line, but she would call me right back. We waited all day, but received no call.

After a short wait at the doctor's office, a nurse comes out to get us, and as we're walking back she says, "Hi, I'm Kristi. Sorry I didn't call you back yesterday; I left early. We had a company picnic and I wasn't sure if it was appropriate to call you from my cell." *Really? That's your excuse? Not appropriate? Woman, I just had cancer. What if I had called because the fluid was leaking and it was purple? Company picnic? Not what I want to hear. Tell me you were called into emergency surgery, and you saved someone's life! I had important questions - I don't care if you called me from a walkie-talkie!*

Anyway, we're here, so let's do this! Katie and I immediately recognize that this nurse has had nine espressos, or has attention deficit disorder, or both. She starts firing off questions, and before I can answer, another question, talking over, around, and up and down!

"Did you take your Cipro two hours before this appointment?" she asked.

"Yes, but I think I was suppose to get two. Dr. Williams said to take one before and one after."

"No, I see here that you had a prescription for one."

"Yes, that's all they gave me when I was discharged from the hospital, but Dr. Williams said to take two."

"No, I see here that your prescription was for one."

"That's because I didn't have my prescription on me when I was discharged, and they only gave me one."

I start to get the feeling that she thinks I'm trying to scam another Cipro. Cipro is an antibiotic. Yeah, I'm trying to cop a Cipro and go on a psychedelic trip! After more back and forth, she goes to ask someone and comes back in and hands me one more Cipro. I tell her that was one of my questions I had when I called yesterday, but she just keeps talking.

She then asks if I brought a diaper. No, that was also one of my questions from the day before. She goes out and brings in this huge thing that would fit Shaquille O'Neal! I'm pretty sure that that if I jumped out of a plane at 12,000 feet, I could use this as a parachute and land without a scratch.

She tells me I will have incontinence, and that I could be normal again in four months. Four months? I don't want to wear this f-ing diaper for four *days*! But I am alive, and that's what matters. I can live with wetting myself. Besides, I sit in traffic a lot, so it might be kind of nice just to let it flow. Flow and go!

She tells me that I could put my underwear over this giant diaper to make it more snug!

"Do you mean boxers?"

"No, briefs."

I laugh. I can't put tighty whities over this giant marshmallow! We go back and forth about this for too many minutes until she finally steps out so I can get undressed. When she returns, Katie asks her about the results from my lymph nodes analysis. We were expecting to get them today. The nurse checks the monitor again and says, "I don't see anything here.

You should get them in, uh, three weeks." Now I know she just made this guesstimation up, but I let it slide. I'm really beginning to think that this woman must've taken an online nursing correspondence course. Maybe the picnic the day before was a celebration of her graduation!

The nurse asks if I've been measuring the fluid from my drain, and was it less than 100 cc per day. I have no idea. She said that I was supposed to be measuring daily. I say, "No one told me."

She says, "Well, you should've measured. Let's check." We approximate that I'm probably leaking approximately 320 cc per day, which is over three times the amount I need before I can have the drain removed. We let her know that was another question we had for her yesterday, had she returned our call. She takes a look at the bandages and removes them. She tells me that she will show me a much better way to dress the drain. She walks over and picks up a gauze and scissors and starts to cut a slit in one of them. She says she will re-bandage it after she removes the catheter.

After I get undressed from the waist down, the nurse instructs me to put a medical mini-blanket over my privates. She begins to explain how this is standard procedure, for my own privacy. Moments later she pulls up the blanket to expose my privates and my lovely catheter coming out of my penis. *Thanks, I feel so much more dignified now.* She begins to take the staples out of my torso, which are stuck, so she pulls harder and comments that she hopes I'd taken my pain meds today. Again, that was another question we had for her yesterday. (I know, I know, the picnic!) I ask her if she can give me a Tylenol.

"No, I'm not allowed to give you any medication."

Oh, I'm sorry, didn't you just hand me Cipro, a prescription drug, just a few minutes ago? She gives up on a few of the staples, commenting, "We'll get back to those. Let's take out the catheter." *Yippee!* She then tells me about a recent patient she had—a big, strong, athletic guy—and when she took out his catheter, he cried. Thank you so much for sharing that little story with me right BEFORE you repeat the same procedure on me!

I then ask yet another question we had for her regarding nutritional supplements and medication. She seems confused. I explain that I work out and take supplements. She cuts me off: "No absolutely not! You cannot work out!" That wasn't my question. Yeah, like I'm going to go do power squats tomorrow. I wanted to ask about whey protein and if would have any effects on my medication. She then wants some fitness advice.

(Two professions that you never want to tell anyone that you do are stand-up comedy and personal training. Every social situation will turn into people wanting weight-loss advice or they want a joke! It usually goes like this: "Hey you're a trainer, what's the best exercise to lose my gut? I reluctantly answer something like, "Increase your cardio exercises, reduce your caloric intake, *blah, blah,*" but no one wants to hear that; they want the quick fix. My answer to their question is usually followed by, "Well I heard about the Ab Buster on an infomercial…!"

Same thing, when people find out I'm a comic. "Hey, tell me a joke…!"

What am I, your monkey? What do you do, oh, you're accountant? Ok, you do my taxes, and I'll do a 5 minute set for you.

The nurse asks me what I think about using her using hiking poles when she does her walks. I just want to get the hell out of there, but I try to offer some advice. Why don't you don't you carry five-pound dumbbells instead? That way you're also toning, and burning more calories as you walk. The bottom line is, are you sweating and sustaining your target heart rate for at least 30 minutes? That's not the answer she wants to hear. She gets defensive: "Well, I used to jog! I saw them on an infomercial! Did I tell you I made a big guy cry recently?"

I want to say to her, "Listen, maybe you just have a 'weight' problem—you can't *wait* to eat!" Ah, snap! Katie, give me a high-five! But, I refrain from this old joke.

Katie has more questions. The nurse instructs her to write them down as a reminder to ask the doctor. Katie doesn't have a pen, so the nutty nurse gives her a Sharpie and a napkin to write them down on. Now have you ever tried to write something on a napkin with a Sharpie? *Houston we have a problem!*

Finally the nurse hears the voice of a surgeon in the hallway, and says she's going to ask him about my drain removal. She goes into the hallway, and asks about removing it. He asks how much I'm draining, and she replies 320 cc every three hours. The door is still half-open so Katie can see the doctor's expression, as I hear his voice raise in immediate concern, "320 cc's every three hours?" Like, "Oh, shit! We've got to get this guy into surgery! Something is really wrong in there!

Katie and I look at each other, and luckily Katie interrupts: "No 320 per day!" The doctor seems relieved, "Well, that's a lot better, but still too much to remove it. It needs to stay in." *Whew! I'm glad we were able to overhear that conversation, or I could be on my way into surgery.*

The nurse strolls back in and continues to remove my hardware. I won't even go into detail about the catheter removal. Just imagine having a garden hose pulled out of your penis. Good times! After more pulling, tugging and cutting, she also gets all of the staples out of my torso. She begins to explain in greater detail what to expect with regard to incontinence, but not before sharing another frightening and irrelevant story. She tells me of an older patient who couldn't control his urine flow after the catheter removal because his urinary tract had been stretched, and then she walks over to the chart to give me an anatomy lesson. After her story, she says, "But he was much older than you." *Well, thanks for sharing, anyway!*

She comes back over to the table with the giant old-man diaper in her hand. She then shows Katie how to properly put it on me. We inform her that we have two babies at home, so we can change diapers with our eyes closed. This information doesn't faze her as she continues to put the diaper on me, "Lift your butt. Now you stick the adhesives on each side." I feel like saying "Goo-goo ga-ga" and peeing in her face!

The nurse instructs me to get dressed, and as I begin, I look down at the exposed drain tube sticking out the side of my body. "Uh, weren't you going to bandage this back up?" She seems perplexed. "Hmmm, yeah, I guess we should…"

Finally, Katie and I get out of there. As I'm waddling to the car with my giant Baby Huey diaper, I wonder what's worse— this old-man's soggy-bottom diaper, or a tube up my penis? It's a close call! We have a two-hour drive home, and as I'm drinking a large beverage, I'm thinking, "Ok, here we go— I'm going to pee myself like an old man. Honey, when we get home, can you change my diaper and give me a shot of Geritol?"

When we eventually get home, I walk straight to the bathroom to pee, or rather, take a look at how much I have already wet myself. It was a hot day, so it was so warm down there wearing this giant diaper that I really couldn't tell if I had, or hadn't. All I know was that I really needed to go now! As I opened my diaper, I was surprised to find that it was completely dry! I had held it for the entire 2 hour ride home! All right! F you, old-man diapers! I begin to pee, and it's a powerful stream! I stop and start several times! I have control! *Damn, I wish there was snow outside so I could go out and write my name in it!*

Let it flow, let it flow, let it flow!

21

Down for the Count

I always feel so guilty, saying goodbye to our kiddos, even though Katie and I will only be gone for two days. Maybe it's because it was so painful for me as a child, when I would have to say goodbye to my dad after a rare visit and never knew when I would see him again. We've been trying to prepare Colin the past couple of days by saying things like, "Do you know who's coming to see you this weekend? Aunt Tina and Uncle Kevin!"

But he replies, "No mmama, dda-da home?" That kid is intuitive! Katie and I have only been away, together, two times since Colin was born. The only babysitters we've had are Katie's parents and Kevin and Tina. (Kevin is Faith's godfather, and Tina is Colin's godmother). To say we're protective of our babies would be an understatement.

As we were getting ready to leave, Colin looks up at me and says, "Da-da doctor?" It takes me a minute, but then I get it—He thinks I'm going back to the hospital because we're all packed up. Oh, man, this is heartbreaking.

I try to reassure him, as I have been doing every day. "No buddy, Da-da's not going back to the doctor; no way!" It's been killing me that I haven't been able to wrestle with him, let alone pick him and Faith up. I tell him that Da-da's booboos are getting much better, and that pretty soon I'll be throwing him high in the air again! This whole experience must be so confusing for him. One day, he and I are at the park, running, climbing and wrestling, and then *boom*! I can't even pick him up. Damn, I've got to get my health back!

Katie has made a lot of plans for our trip to Newport Beach this weekend: whale watching, Balboa Island, dinner both nights with her cousin Brian and his girlfriend, and more. Oh, yeah, I'm also supposed to do a lot of writing! This is supposed to be our last big hoorah before I go back to work. I've been recovering for three weeks, and Monday it's back in the saddle! Actually, that's a bad analogy, because I am definitely not ready to ride in a saddle. However, I'm training some clients Monday, and have my follow-up pitch with the Encore network on Monday. My first pitch with Encore was just myself and Rob Eric from Scout Productions. Apparently it went well, because now they want Tommy Lee and his team there for this pitch. I really need to need to go in there and rock this meeting! I also have a pitch with Comedy Central on Wednesday. My big comeback!

Newport Beach is a cool little surf town about an hour south of Los Angeles. It's a totally different vibe than where we live. Everyone is so laid back, riding around on their beach cruisers, jogging and surfing. The locals really soak up life! That 80s song *Walking in L.A.* is true—nobody walks in LA. We have gyms where people valet park! You drive to the gym, and valet because you're too lazy to park and walk into the gym to get on the treadmill to walk. Besides, it just doesn't look cool to walk! L.A. people want to roll up to the front in their Mercedes, to be noticed. Katie has been taking care of me and our kiddos for three weeks, so this Newport Beach trip is just what the doctor ordered. Actually Brian, Katie's cousin, set it up for us. The law firm where he works has a sweet deal on some beach houses, so he offered us a great little place for the weekend and we're more than happy to take him up on it.

We arrive and get settled in. We're in the upper level of a beach house right on the sand. It's obviously a sweet spot, because there are surfers right in front of our place. It's a pretty chilly weekend, but that's OK; we're just happy to get a little escape. Katie has spoken to Brian, and the plan is for him and his girlfriend to come over for some wine before we head out to dinner. For some reason, the past two or three years I've been having a very strange, adverse reaction to alcohol. I attributed it to my sinuses, until I received this cancer news. Now I'm beginning to think it's all related. My body can't process toxins, or something to that effect. About a week before my surgery, I meet a friend out for a quick dinner and drinks. I only had two beers, but spent the next day miserable and throwing up! What the F? I use to pound vodkas-tonics all night long at Skybar, then wake up at 5:00 a.m. and hit the gym. Something strange is going on with my system. I'm very aware of this as we go into our weekend, so my game plan is to take it easy, and just try to hang in there. Brian and his girlfriend, Liz, arrive around 8:00 p.m., and I open a special bottle that Katie and I have brought from a winery that we stayed at in Carmel Valley, BK (before kiddos).

We're all chatting and having a great time, when everyone but me decides to have a refill. I decide to hold off and continue to nurse my chardonnay. First of all, it's not very manly to even drink chardonnay, but the fact that I can't even handle a couple of glasses is very emasculating!

On the way to dinner, the weather turns very bizarre. It starts storming –thunder, lightning and hail! Highly unusual. I should've taken this as a sign. We stop by the grocery store and grab two bottles of wine for the restaurant, since the corkage fee is only 4 dollars. All the while, I'm thinking to myself, "OK, maybe I'll have one more glass, and I know three of them can handle the rest." I prefer red wine, but the results from that have been even worse for me. What a puss!

We arrive at the restaurant, but our table isn't ready so we're told to wait at the bar. *OK, "Wait" doesn't mean "Have a drink."* Oh, is that Brian ordering us a round? Shit! I step in because I can't let him pay! He already has gotten us the beach house and insisted on dinner tonight. I agreed only if I can pick up the tab the next night! For some dumb reason, I order a vodka-tonic, just like the good old days. Katie sees this and starts grilling me about the plans we have for this weekend, etc. She knows the consequences if I drink one too many or mix my alcohols. I assure her it's all good— I'm either going to nurse this one through dinner, or not drink it and just have a little more chardonnay. We get seated and I order a French dip sandwich. Since Brian is paying, I don't want to take advantage of him and get a pricier dinner, although I know something lighter will be better for my system. Since researching cancer, Katie and I have discovered that meat increases the risk of cancer. This is a tough one for me, especially being from BBQ-famous Kentucky, I love meat! I grill two or three times a week! Besides, I don't eat fish. Oh, I also had a large beef burger for lunch. *Can you say "glutten for punishment?"*

Katie and I have decided to only have meat a few times a month. I reassure her we'll be starting our new program on Monday. Over the course of dinner, I stick to my word and nurse the vodka, drinking less than half, but I also have about 1 ½ glasses of wine. I feel fine and hope for the best. As Brian drives us back to our place, he decides to go over Balboa Island to avoid the police. Brian is an attorney at a respected firm down here, so a D.U.I. would not go over well. Katies' sisters, Colleen and Erin, both used to work on Balboa, so we will be driving past their old place of employment, a bar called the Village Inn. As we pass the place, someone makes a remark about stopping in, and unfortunately for me, a car pulls out of a spot right in the front. I try to dissuade this decision, but no one pays much attention as Brian continues to parallel park. Uh, oh, there's no excuse now, so we go in for a few minutes. Again I order a vodka drink, with the same intention—fake the funk! Just nurse the damn thing, which I do.

Although we're having a good time, I'm well aware that this is probably not the best situation for my system, but I don't want to be a spoilsport, so I decide to hang in there. Luckily we're only there about 15 minutes when the bar announces last call, even though it's only midnight. OK, I might be safe; let's head back so I can hit the sheets and recharge. As we're heading back, I can feel the headache starting to creep on me. Shit, this is not good! This is our special weekend! As we enter our beach pad, I inform Katie of this fact and tell her it will be fine, I'm just going to take half of a Norco and sleep it off. Norco is the pain pill that was prescribed to me following my surgery. Since the pills had made me so nauseous after my surgery, I was not planning on taking more, but tonight I have no choice. I swallow the pill and hit the bed. Around 4:30 a.m., I awaken with a strong need to use the restroom! Since my surgery I'm very paranoid of losing my bladder control while sleeping, so I spring out of bed and dash to the bathroom. The bathroom is down a very short hallway from our bedroom, and being the Southern gentleman that I am, I close the door behind me. As I'm standing there doing my business, I begin to feel very light-headed and dizzy. The next thing I know, it feels like someone cracks me in the middle of my spine with a 2x4, and smashed in my head with a brick! I don't know what just happened, but it hurt—a lot! I had apparently fallen backwards hitting my back on the edge of the counter and then, falling to my right, hit my head on the tile floor. *Timber!*

I struggle to open my eyes as I hear someone in the distance yelling my name. Turns out, it's not in the distance; it's Katie, sounding terrified, and banging on the bathroom door. As I begin to come to, I notice that for some reason, I'm lying on the cold, hard floor facing the bathtub. I immediately jump up, dazed and confused, and open the door. I don't remember who spoke first, but she has since told me I said, "I think I just passed out!" Right after I say this, she my eyes roll into the back of head and I start falling straight backwards. She grabs my head to protect it and goes down with me. She said she was yelling for me to wake up, but I was not responding. She runs to find her cell phone to call 911. I apparently wake up before she dials, and I yell to her that I'm OK! I have never seen fear in Katie's eyes like this before! I'm also very proud and don't want her to see me like this, so when she gets back to the bathroom, I'm on my feet again.

I have no recollection of what I said this time, but the same thing happened again! As I slur my words, trying to convince her that I'm fine, my eyes roll into the back of my head and I'm going down again! Once again, Katie saves me from cracking my head open on the tile floor by catching me and going down with me! I'm out for count, once again. This is the third time. Now if I were a boxer, this is the part where my trainer would be in the corner yelling, "Just stay down! Stay down, you idiot!" I come to again and decide to listen to my imaginary trainer this time, and stay down. I yell for Katie again, and tell her I'm fine! Katie is a very smart lady, but it doesn't take a Rhodes Scholar to figure out that a man passing out three times in a row is not fine. This time I decide to crawl to where she is in the living room. My heart is racing and I am sweating profusely. I plead with her not to call 911, and ask her to please just get me some water. I pull off my shirt and throw it on the couch, as I start guzzling the water. I can't stop thinking about our kids, especially Colin, since he's older, and how it would scare him if I go to the hospital again. I promised him when we left, "Da-Da's not going to the doctor, no way!" I also start to imagine how disappointed people would be in me. I can hear them saying, "Wait, he's been recovering from cancer surgery for only three weeks, and he goes out, drinks, and takes a pain pill and passes out? What a dumb ass!"

My mouth is so dry, I can't drink enough to quench my thirst. After about 15 minutes, Katie and I go back to bed. I put my shirt back on and lie next to her. I, unfortunately, had just read an interview in *Esquire* magazine with Liam Neeson two nights ago. In the interview, he talked about his wife, actress Natasha Richardson's, tragic death. Natasha died of a head injury that she received while skiing two years earlier. She hit her head and seemed fine afterwards, but died a few hours later from swelling of the brain. I also remember something about not going to sleep if you have a concussion. I hear sirens and start thinking that maybe the people downstairs had heard all of the commotion and called the cops. Damn, now I'll have to explain everything to them and they'll call an ambulance for sure! Luckily the cops weren't coming for us. I lie awake a couple more hours and finally dose off. Around 7:30, I waken with a sudden urge to throw up. Uh, oh! I barely make it to the bathroom. Let me just say, the hamburger, the prime rib French dip and the wine all came up very fast and furiously! This was not going to be a fun day for the D-man. I return to bed and give Katie the news—no whale watching for me, but I insist she still go. I feel like a complete idiot for screwing our trip up.

Katie goes whale watching with Brian and his girlfriend, while I spend the day violently throwing up. Sunday morning comes around and I'm feeling a little more human, but now I'm a lot more aware of my injuries from the falls. Let's just work our way up my body—my right ankle is sore, I have a knot on the side of my calf, my right hip hurts, the middle of my spin has a bruise, my back has all sorts of markings, my neck is stiff, and I have two knots on my head! This so-called relaxing weekend has beaten the hell out of me! Katie and I have a nice breakfast with Brian on Balboa Island before we head home.

Oh, I almost forgot to mention that my sister Donna texted me and gave me a heads-up that my mom will be arriving in a town about 15 minutes from me tomorrow with SFB (her husband) in the 18-wheeler truck. Supposedly they will get a rental car and he will bring her to see me and our family, while he stays in a motel for three days. Hmm....where have I heard this before? Oh, yes, every other time they've come out here! Here's his M.O.—SFB tells my mom that they will be 15 minutes from my house (it doesn't matter if it's Fontana, Barstow or San Diego)! Any one of these places is hours from my house, but my mom doesn't know the difference. I call my sister, Sandy, to confirm the story, and ask her about the rental car-motel story, which I didn't believe anyway. Sandy informs me that this can't be possible because neither one of them even has a credit card. Damn! I knew it was a set-up! If I don't drop everything to come and see her, I will look like I'm the bad guy, and SFB will remind her of this for years to come. Never mind that this is my first time back to work in three weeks— I have two very important network pitches. And, oh yeah, I'M RECOVERING FROM CANCER! Shit! This stresses me out every time it happens!

Monday morning, as I'm working, sure enough, I get a call from my mom. I hate speaking to her when SFB is around because she's very timid and doesn't make a lot of sense. Also, when she is talking on the phone with anyone, he is always ranting about some nonsense in the background. I've told her to tell him I said it's rude to talk while someone is on the phone and to shut up, but she nervously laughs and ignores me. She tells me they will be dropping a load off at LAX at 7:00 Tuesday morning, and from there they will be going to Barstow for a few days to wait for the next load. OK, I tell my mom, I will cancel my appointments for Tuesday morning to come and pick HER up (she knows he will never be welcome in our home or around my children). I explain I can drive her back out to Barstow on

Thursday. She says that will work, and that she will call me that afternoon to give me the address. I don't hear from her until 4:30 the next afternoon. OK, new plan—Now they are in Ontario, California, so we make arrangements for me to pick her up Thursday and take her back there on Saturday. Shit, here we go again!

Katie has plans this week, but changes everything because my mom will supposedly be staying with us. I tell Katie not to hold her breath. I decide to wait until the day my mom's visit to start preparing Colin for it. By the way, my mom has never met our daughter, Faith, and Colin has only seen her twice—once when he was five weeks old, and once when Katie and I took him to Kentucky when he was a year and a half. Even though I've shown Colin pictures to remind him, I don't believe he understands our relationship to her.

In the meantime, Tommy Lee didn't make our Monday afternoon pitch with Encore. I get the news that he's not coming, just as I arrive, but try to remain calm and confident. The pitch goes pretty well, despite the chaos going thru my head. We move forward!

Tuesday I decide to hit the gym, even though the doctor said to wait six weeks. I say, "Three weeks, and that's my final offer." I decide to do a light warm- up on the recumbent bike, but I discover the pedaling motion is killing my groin area. I only last one minute. I do better on the machines, lifting very light weights, while keeping my core stabilized. There is always a lot of testosterone in the gym. I see some guys working out, thinking they are bad-asses, and it's killing me! I want to sling some iron, but here I am lifting these girlie-man weights! *Damn, I should be at Curves, the gym for chubby girls!* (By the way, Big bottom girls make the rockin world go round). I want to have a t-shirt made that reads, "I'm not a pussy, I just had cancer!"

Wednesday is another action-packed day and I have another pitch scheduled, this time with Comedy Central. I'm trying to stay focused and keep my eye on the prize. I double-checked the evening before, and yes, Tommy Lee and his manger are confirmed for the pitch! Whew! OK, let's do this! I've been hustling the last 48 hours trying to get numbers together for our budget. I've been calling friends that have had HBO and Comedy Central specials, so I'm excited to pass all of this information along to Rob Eric at Scout, which I do via emails, but I receive nothing from him, not even a courtesy response. Nice team work!

One hour before the meeting I find out that Tommy and his manger will not be at the pitch. S.O.B.! I've been waiting a year-and-a-half to lock down our rock star host of the show, and now he's not showing up for the pitches. I only get one shot at this! I try to remain calm and loose, all the while things continue to change with my mom! Now she says she can only stay for one night! *OK, just breathe and focus. Ohmmmm!*

As Rob, Jenna (Tommy's publicist) and I sit in the conference room at MTV/Comedy Central waiting for the executives, I decide to bring up the emails I sent to Rob and call him a dick. Nice timing! He claims that he didn't get them. Hmm…the old "lost in cyberspace" excuse, huh? After 45 minutes and still no sign of the execs, we (well, Rob) decide to pull a power move and leave. We tell the assistant that we want to reschedule. Now this is a cool move if you have actual power in this town! This is my first big project, so I need this network more than they need me. Regardless, we reschedule. I hope this works!

Thursday morning, as I'm reading to Colin, I finally decide to tell him about my mom's visit. "Do you know who's coming to see us today? Mam-maw! Do you remember her? She's your other grandmother. She's Da-Da's mommy!"

Colin looks confused, but nods like he remembers. The plan is for me to work until 3:00 p.m. and then start the two-hour drive to pick up my mom. Katie thinks I'm insane, but I try to explain that, even though I'll be in traffic for hours, I will be alone with my mom which is very rare. At around 10:00 a.m., I get a message from her. Now she can't even spend the night, but she still wants me to drive out and see her. It's the same old B.S.—SFB won't allow her to even spend the night to see her son, who's recovering from cancer, or her grandkids!

I make it to the T/A truck stop in Ontario in just under two hours. The seatbelt presses right against my wounds, so I can't wait to get out of this car. I've Googled restaurants in the area. My plan is to pick her up and take her off the truckstop grounds.

I decide to take her to an Olive Garden, a hell of a lot nicer than a truck stop, but not so fancy that she will feel out of place. I've called her cell to tell her that I'm only a few exits away, and when I pull in, I see her waiting outside the truckstop. My mom is so worried about everyone else that she can't even relax for the five minutes it would take me to get there from the exit.

I tell her my plan to kidnap her and take her out to eat, but I can tell that this makes her extremely nervous. She keeps insisting that we can eat at the truck stop. She tells me that SFB is sitting outside. I think she's nervous to be out of his sight. I tell her that I didn't come all this way to see him. I ask her for a restroom and she leads me to one close to the door where she had said he was. I go in thinking she will go out and tell him that I'm here, and she will come back in and then we can go somewhere and be alone to talk. As I come out of the bathroom, she's standing there waiting for me. She wants me to walk with her outside. I should have remembered the routine— for the hundredth time, she's going to try to get me to chit-chat with this abusive asshole. She starts walking out the door to where he is sitting, before I can argue with her. Actually, I realize this is fine, because my plan is, if he even gives my mom or me attitude, I'm going to slap the shit out of him, cancer or no cancer.

I know misery loves company so, for the last 10 years or so, when I visit, I have always chosen to be "on" to really irritate him. I speak and laugh louder than normal and I give my mom lots of attention, because I know it kills him! He usually tries to pretend that it doesn't bother him, but I can tell it does. Also, after I leave, I get reports from my sisters that my mom is paying the price by receiving his verbal abuse, and that's what is in front of others. I'm sure it's even worse when my mom and SFB are out of sight. Mom and I walk out onto the patio area and there he is, in all of his misery, sulking as usual. He pretends not to notice us as we walk right toward him. My mom says something about how I finally made it, as we approach him.

Wow, what a surprise. He doesn't say anything, not even, "Hey, how are you feeling? Sorry you had to drive all the way out here right after your cancer operation!" What an evil motherfucker. I decide to kick off the conversation and see how he wants it to go. I say, in a matter-of-fact kind of way, "What's up?" He mumbles something inaudible, looks my way, and moves his hand like he expects mine to be there to shake, but it's not. I just stare at him coldly. I can tell my mom is very tense about this because she continues talking nervously about nothing. Right before Colin was born (Katie was due any minute), I had to drive out to one of these far-away shithole truck stops just to see her for 15 minutes. On that visit, I confronted him about his anger issues toward my mom. He pouted and walked away, climbed up on his truck to piddle around with it, and then shouted to my mom, "Nelda, Stevie thinks I'm mean to you! When have I ever been mean to you?" He sounded like a 12-year-old!

I wanted to say, "Only for the last 30 years you, fucking coward." But I knew he would just let her have it as soon I left, and she had a very long truck ride back to Kentucky and God knows where else, so I looked at my mom and told her not to answer, and kept right on talking to her, ignoring his childish remark.

He stands up and makes some excuse about needing to check on his truck and walks away. My mom tells him that we will be inside, at the restaurant! So much for taking her away for an hour or two. I spend the next 90 minutes eating in front of my mom (they ate an hour before I got here, even though I told her I was taking her to dinner). As we make small talk, I show her pictures of Colin and Faith, hoping that maybe should she will come to her senses and say, "Let's get out of here and go see my grandbabies; I can fly home next week!" But, of course, that was a silly fantasy, and it didn't happen. At exactly 6:00 p.m., I inform her I have to get on the road in order to make it back to read to Colin for his bedtime. She doesn't even walk me back to my car, and we exchange an awkward one-arm side-hug in the entrance of the truck stop. I've had valet attendants give me warmer hugs. As I walk back to my car, I wonder when I will see her again. I can't wait get to home to my loving, peaceful, drama-free home. I call Katie and have her tell Colin that Da-Da will make it home in time to read his bedtime story, and I am.

23

Tommy Lee

HBO— this is the big dance! We are meeting with Michael Lombardo, the president of the network. It's "go" time baby, and look who decided to show up—Tommy! Tommy is exactly how you think he would be in person--tall, gangly and full of energy. He bounces around like a little kid! Although I dig his vibe, I hope he is ready to step up and sell this show. Tommy is accompanied by his manager and his marketing person. From the Scout Productions team, it's two of the partners, Rob and Michael. We are led down a long hallway and into a beautiful corner conference room. I learn that this was the former office of the previous president of HBO, Chris Albrecht, who departed the company in an unceremonious manner involving lawsuits and name-calling. We are told that because of the situation, no one would use this office in fear that there could be bad energy attached, so they decided to convert it into a conference room. We will be the very first pitch in this newly redecorated room. I wish I knew a chant for good karma. Our team sits on one side of the table with our backs to the window. I'm never quite sure where to sit in these meetings. Is there a strategy or protocol involved? I have no idea. I'm always afraid the executive is going to walk in and think, "Who the fuck does this guy think he is sitting in my spot? There's no way I'm going to buy a show from this dipshit!"

We are seated at a huge, mahogany table that is shining like a brand new Rolls Royce that has just come off the assembly line. As we wait, the assistant asks the customary question, "Can I get someone a drink?" Of course I'm thinking to myself, *"Yes, Tommy and I will take a few shots of Patrón! Let's get this party started!"* I have no idea what's about to happen, since we didn't discuss any sort of strategy before going in.

I remember seeing the famous picture of Ozzy Osbourne, smiling while holding the body of the white dove as blood trickled from his mouth. The story behind the photo is that after Ozzy had sabotaged his health and career with years of drug abuse, his wife, Sharon, became his manager and orchestrated his amazing comeback. After recording his new album, Ozzy had a meet-and-greet with his new bosses at the record company as a chance to get to know each other. Ozzy decided to show up wasted and release a bag of white doves in the conference room. After releasing the doves, Ozzy sits on the lap of one of the female executives, grabs one of the doves and bites its head off to the shock and horror of the executives. Hey, they don't call him the Prince of Darkness for nothing!

Is Tommy going to pull a similar stunt? When Michael Lombardo takes a seat, is Vince Neil going to bust down the door on his Harley with 14 strippers behind him just like in the Girls, Girls, Girls video? I hope so! Let's leave them something to remember us by! Unfortunately, this is the opposite of what the geniuses from Scout Productions had in mind. The only rock n' roll moment of the meeting was after Michael and his assistant came in, we all introduced ourselves, but were unable to shake hands because of this huge, Titanic-size table. This was unacceptable for Tommy, who promptly flung his body across the table, scratching the shiny finish with his belt buckle along the way. Way to christen the ship, bro! At least they'll have a cool story to tell about the scratch.

As Rob began the pitch, I knew we were in trouble. I have been on many pitches with Rob, but this was the first time I has seen him rattled and insecure. He seemed very nervous as he explained how this would be an alternative comedy show, with a "loungey" feel. He compared it to the show from the late 60s and 70s, *Playboy After Dark*, with guests mingling around while the comic performed. Some of the guests, he explained, may even have their backs to the comic. *Is he fucking nuts? That's a comic's worst nightmare!* Nothing will drive a comedian crazier than someone in the audience not paying attention, or even worse, talking during the set! Has this guy ever been to a comedy club in his life? Also, he says that not all of the comics will do well; some may even bomb. Some may have never even been on stage before. At this point, I'm about to get up and go kick him in his fucking throat! *I've worked on this project for six years, and now, after a year of negotiations, we have Tommy Lee sitting in the room and you're pitching a fucking coffee house open-mic night show?* Scout Production is responsible for creating *Queer Eye for the Straight Guy*, among other design shows, so I shouldn't be too surprised that their vision of ROC is more artsy than mine, but still, I am!

Michael Lombardo expresses doubts about this type of format. I watch as Tommy is then questioned by Michael Lombardo, but attempts to play along. I get the feeling that he's thinking the same thing I am—*How the fuck is this a rock-comedy concert?* Bingo night at the Elk's Club sounds more dangerous this. I jump in to try and save this sinking ship, but it's too late! I explain to Michael that this show will be based on the DVD, and he asks, "What DVD?" Way to have a concise plan, Scout! *United we stand, divided we suck!* Where are Vince Neil and those strippers?

HBO passes on Rockstars of Comedy.

Stevie D. and Tommy Lee

24

Livin' On a Prayer, I'm halfway There!

The results from my six-month PSA test once again read .01%. I'm not quite sure what that means, but I think it's good. So, here we are once again in this armpit of a city, Riverside, California. I really hope I never see this town again, after all of this is said and done. I think I'm a little more relaxed this time around. I don't get to see Dr. Williams very often, so I want to make the most of this visit.

As I sit in the waiting area, I notice that once again, it's me along with a room full of old dudes. After a brief wait in his office, in walks Dr. Williams, all smiles and with a reassuring demeanor. I don't remember exactly what questions I asked that day, but one I remember specifically is, "Why am I still doing the PSA test when I no longer have a prostate?" Dr. Williams explains that if my PSA were to be high that would mean the cancer has spread to another part of my body. He tells me the bad thing is that it's an early detection technique so they still wouldn't know where the cancer is, even though it shows up in the PSA-count. Cancer is a fucking coward—show yourself, you sneaky bastard! For the record, that last line is my own thought, not a direct quote from Dr. Williams.

I can't believe it's only been six months. I have to say that this has been the hardest time of my adult life. I am back in full swing, busting my ass more than ever, but I seem to be spinning my wheels a lot of the time. I don't talk about cancer, I just want to get as healthy as possible and pick up the pieces. I stopped doing standup to focus on being a producer and stay close to my family, but I am starting to panic, thinking, "What will I do if this doesn't work out?" My contract with Scout Productions and Tommy Lee ends in October, I have got to hustle and get another project going in case of the very real possibility that Scout fucks this up.

November, 2011

A few months ago, I started working on my backup plan, creating more reality shows to pitch. Some of these ideas come at me at night when I'm lying awake; others are brought to me via my agent, Christine. It usually goes like this: Christine will call and say she has a client, such as three-time Ultimate Fighting Championship (UFC) champ Rich Franklin, and I will then brainstorm to come up with a concept for him. This is a new ballgame for me. After years of being on stage or in front of the camera, I'm now going into meetings at networks and trying to convince them that I know what the hell I'm doing. Here are just a few examples of projects that have been my brain child:

Hot Rod Heroes, starring hot rod Builder of the Year Troy Ladd

Attitude Adjustment 101, starring three-time UFC champ Rich Franklin

The Sting, starring renowned ATF agent and bad-ass Jay Dobyns

There are more, but these are at the forefront right now. I like all of my projects to have an edge, a reflection of my brand. Unfortunately, my brain cannot rest, so I lie awake at night creating and worrying. I read once that Walt Disney had gone to a psychic who told him he would die at 35. After hearing this, Walt became a workaholic, even popping in to spy on his animators at all hours of the night. I can relate to Walt, not because I've visited some kook who read tarot cards. (By the way, have you noticed that all of the psychics have neon signs outside of their place of business? Do people think, "You know, I was skeptical at first, but then I saw the fancy neon sign, so there must be a professional in there reading that crystal ball!" Anyway, I don't believe in that hocus pocus.) Case in point:

Katie was pregnant with Colin and we were house shopping. This was in 2008, when there were a lot of foreclosed homes with loans that were given to dipshits that couldn't make their payments once their adjustable rate kicked in. We decided that on our budget we could either buy a condo in a decent area, or we could buy a house in a shitty neighborhood. I'm a good ol' boy— just give me a yard and a BBQ grill and I'm good to go. Shots fired? Police helicopters? Who cares—check out these tri-tips I'm firing up!

So we were, house hunting and finding some very strange places. The houses were either vandalized because the tenants left very angrily, or they were very sketchy, with shoddy, temporary walls erected to accommodate multiple families (typical illegal housing situation). By the way, our Realtor would not even meet us in these neighborhoods to show us the homes. We were getting discouraged and about to give up when we decided to try one more. We arrived at a decent-looking, mid -century house only to find that the key given to us didn't work because the former tenant had changed the locks.

We walked around the house and it really didn't look that bad, although I felt guilty when I looked in the window and saw children's toys that had been left behind. As we approached the backyard, I saw something surprising– a school bus sitting in the yard. And then it hit me— additional families had been living in there. "Hey, Katie, check it out—a guest house!" Katie wasn't amused, and asked how we could even get rid of it. Good question—how do you get a fucking bus out of your backyard?

Next, I noticed a strange-looking, octagonal-shaped building. At first I thought, "Right on! Storage, or better yet, a man cave!" But as we got closer, I noticed there were crude-looking animal pelts over the door and two spears at the entrance. What the F? As I cautiously approach, I hear Katie shout, "Don't go in there!" I ignore her and enter to find a freaky scene! There was an altar with fake skulls and other Voodoo-looking shit in there, along with what appeared to be blood splattered all over the walls! I picked up a skull on a stick and began shaking it. I went outside the building holding it while doing a impromptu sacrificial dance. At this point, Katie was freaking out and started running to the car, screaming, "That's not funny, that's Santería!"

"That's what? Sangria? Cool! Let's have a few and do some dirty Voodoo dancing!"

Katie shouts that's she's leaving me there, because this was a Santería house, and explains briefly, while sprinting, that it's a form of Mexican-Caribbean witchcraft! There has been a spell put on this house! I was still laughing and cracking jokes as I chased her. "Can we get an additional 10% off with that?" Luckily we did not have Rosemary's baby after that incident, or buy the house, but I did put an offer in on the bus.

Sorry, once again, I digress. So where was I? Oh, yeah, I was talking about getting my hustle back on after this bump in the road. Unlike, my single days in L.A., I now have a family to support in a town with 50,000 others trying to do the same thing as me! Bring it on, 'cause the D-man does not quit! We'll see who's the last comic, rock star, producer, super dad standing! OK, there's my pep talk for today. Now I'll just wait for the phone to ring like every other wannabe in this town.

25

November 16

I have an appointment with Dr. Ravari, my general doctor, whom I haven't seen since this all went down. I had last seen Dr. Ravari in early 2010, when I had my physical. She had then instructed me to come back in for my blood work, which I blew off, until I received my reminder in November, 2010. Dr. Ravari had been out on maternity leave, so we're just catching up. We have a lot to talk about, but my main reason for this visit today is to have some moles checked out. I have never done this before, but like I said, cancer is a sneaky bastard, so I'm just trying to stay one step ahead. Also, I've had what seems to be a rash on my back. I feel like aliens have taken over my body. After catching up, she examines my back. I really like Dr. Ravari. She's very personable and patient with me. She informs me that the rash on back is a fungus and gives me a prescription. *A fungus?* Damn! Tis just keeps getting better. How hot is that? I can only imagine if I were single right now and trying to pick up a girl.

"Hi, I'm Steve, I'm only in my forties, but I've had prostate cancer this year, and now a skin fungus. What time should I pick you up? And, oh yeah, did I mention the moles?"

So it turns out that the fungus is probably caused by my sweaty workout clothes, and I find out a few days later that the moles she was most concerned with were benign.

Dr. Ravari reminds me that I have two more PSA tests to do before March 1st, but she is ordering an additional blood test, as well, that could detect the sneaky bastard lurking around somewhere else. This lady knows her stuff.

A few days later, I drop off some vegetarian chili (compliments of Katie) to my agent and friend, Christine, who is recovering from a hysterectomy. Christine had a double mastectomy five years ago, and now she was strongly urged to have her ovaries removed, since she was at a very high risk of the cancer returning there. Her mother, she and I are discussing Christine's recovering when Christine tells her mom that I'm also a "survivor." This announcement makes me very uncomfortable. Not once in these eight months since my surgery have I described myself as a "survivor," but I guess that's what I am. And I plan to keep on surviving for a long, long time.

I had first met Christine through my friend and former agent, Brando. Brando was a cool, laid-back guy, always smiling and ready to do a shot of booze or partake in some herb. Christine and Brando had been married and worked in the talent same agency, before they divorced. After my DVD *Rockstars of Comedy* came out, I brought Brando onboard to help me pitch it as a weekly television show. Brando loved the project, and everything rock-related. He grew up in Northern California and was childhood friends with the band Green Day. He was proud of this fact and talked about his old friends a lot. He had told the guys all about ROC, so when Green Day came to L.A. to play, he was stoked and really wanted me to go to the show with him. I like Green Day, but I'm not a big enough fan to drag my ass out on a school night, especially since I felt like I'd only slept about four hours total since Colin was born. However, Brando was so excited that I didn't want to let him down, so I told him I would go, if I could drive separately and meet him there.

I was bitching and moaning all the way there. The traffic sucked. I even got lost and almost turned around to go home. I ended up sticking it out and I'm so glad I did. I had never seen Brando so excited as he was at that concert. He was running around like a kid in a candy store. We had some seats that were pretty good to me, but apparently not good enough for Brando, so he called the band's manager—another childhood friend— who immediately came to get us and took us backstage. After slamming a couple of Heinekens backstage, we went out to the concert to check out the show. Brando was jumping around like a maniac, singing at the top of his lungs and chest bumping as Green Day rocked. I tried a couple of times to have a conversation with Brando, but he was flying too high to comprehend. He was having an amazing time, but I did notice that he was pretty wasted, also. I haven't gone out much lately, not even many comedy gigs, but on the few occasions recently that I had been out with Brando, he was definitely up for a good time—a much better time than me.

Brando and I have been spending a lot of time lately working on *Rockstars*, having meetings, lunches, and talking on the phone at least five times a day. He always seems to be positive and motivated, except for a couple of conversations we had the previous week, when he seemed distressed over some personal and professional issues. But I was getting a kick out of seeing him beaming with pride this on this night. The highlight of the evening was when Green Day's singer, Billy Joe Armstrong, told a story about a night out with Brando. I was familiar with this story because, just the week before, Brando has sent me a video of Billy Joe telling this story to a sold out show at Madison Square Garden. Brando didn't want to seem like he was bragging, so he didn't tell me what the video was. He would just ask every day if I had seen it. Since I didn't know what the hell it was, I didn't want to invest the five minutes to watch. Finally I watched, and told Brando how fucking cool it was. I could tell this made him very proud, and validated his relationship with the band.

As the band was sharing the story, the manager I had met earlier, and another old friend and employee of the band, came to find us as we whooped it up with the man of the hour, Brando. We even got to capture this Kodak moment, thanks to my Blackberry. Unfortunately, the picture is blurry. In between his dancing around and trips to grab more beers, he would mention how cool the after-party was going to be. Little did he know, I had no intention of staying for it. The concert was nearing the end, and you can always tell when a band is going to do an encore when you can think of one or two of their biggest hits that they haven't performed yet.

Brando had just taken off on a beer run again, when I decided I was going leave and beat the crowd. I waited for him to return for a few minutes, but decided that in his state of mind, there would probably be no reasoning with him, concerning my decision to go, so I just cut out. As soon as I got in my car, I tried to call him and apologize, but his phone went to voicemail.

The next morning as I was getting ready to leave for work, I told Katie all about the show, and how excited Brando was all night. I was tired from little sleep, but I was so glad I went. I waited a few hours before I made my first call of the day. Brando would usually answer in great spirits and say his usual phrase, "Yes, sir!" (With a high emphasis on the "Yes") I can still hear him saying it like it was yesterday. His enthusiasm about ROC really fired me up! I waited an hour or two before I placed another call to him. We were supposed to meet around noon to sign a contract from our lawyer that I had with me in my car. The second call was unanswered. On my third message, I joked about him being hungover, and told him I could meet him anywhere; I just needed his signature. When I got home that evening, I told Katie that I had a bad feeling about not hearing from Brando. I was afraid that maybe he had gotten a D.U.I. At around 6:30 p.m., I got a call from Danielle, a friend of Brando's, who had ridden with him to the concert. She seemed to be sobbing. "Brando's dead."

She didn't know any details. Apparently the manager for Green Day, Steve, had called to give her the news but would not divulge any other details. After I hung up with her, I made a phone call and got the truth. He had taken his life by hanging himself in his garage, after a heated fight with Christine, his ex-wife. Brando's loss devastated me. I had so many emotions running through my body—sadness, anger, confusion, guilt! After milling it over in my brain a million times, all I can think is that Brando just got too wasted and made a very stupid mistake that he could not take back. I miss you so much, buddy. Until we meet again, keeping rockin'!

26

Hammer Time!

(Disclaimer: I was a little bitter when I wrote this chapter. *Ohmmm.*)

So, just in case I haven't come out and said directly that this has been a difficult year, let me make it clear—this has been an extremely difficult year and it's just gotten difficult-er! A production deal with E One Entertainment on my project with Rich Franklin was just scrapped. This deal was my saving grace after Scout Productions fudged up my other two shows. The stress is making it almost impossible for me to sleep. I lie awake at night with a million thoughts running through my head. Between waking at 5:00 a.m., training, meetings, creating shows, and being a full-time dad, I'm pulling 18 to 19-hour days. I wish I had a cut-off switch for my brain so I can get some shut-eye to recharge my batteries. Some days I feel like I make a Wall Street trader look like a Zen Monk. I hope I don't short circuit. *Ohmmm.*

I've heard that God only gives us as much as he knows we can handle. Okay, God, I hope I've met my quota, because "I'm about to lose my mind up in here, up in here." See, I must be going bonkers, because I'm quoting rapper DMX.

E One had been expressing, over and over, how excited they were about the Rich Franlin project. After negotiating Rich's fee and credits for the show, we were supposedly done, and just waiting on the contracts to be sent over. I starting getting a little nervous, because I hadn't heard from them, so I had Christine put the pressure on them, to see what the hold-up was. Since the producer at E One was my contact, he called me first to break the bad news. Apparently the execs at the networks were now only looking for family-based reality shows. There is a very high turnover rate for network execs, so it's much safer to wait for shows on other networks to become hits, and then copy them. *American Idol* is a hit, so let's create 40 other shows that are the exact same format—*The Voice, X Factor, America's Got Talent*—all the same fucking show! There is no creativity anymore.

By the way, speaking of these variety-type live shows, about seven years ago, Arleen Sorkin asked me what I thought would be the next format of hit shows, and I predicted live variety shows— the kind that the whole family could sit around and enjoy. She said that if I would shoot something, she would help me shop it. Since I obviously didn't have the resources to film a huge production in front of a live audience, I shot a pilot in front of a green screen (which allows other video or graphics to be added later), with myself as the host, introducing the performers on video. I spent months gathering tapes from comics, dancers, singers, and other acts. After editing and re-editing, we finally had a cut that Arleen and I liked. She screened it for her kids and some friends in their private screening room. I screened it for my nieces and nephews and some of their parents. I wanted to get responses from both age groups. Both screenings went very well, so Arleen decided to show it to a good friend of hers (I'll call him Allen). Allen had produced several sketch comedy and stand-up comedy shows. The feedback I got from him was that I should film it inside a trailer, like I was a jobless redneck, and introduce the acts as if I were watching them on my TV. *"Hey, I'm just a dipshit hillbilly, drinking my Pabst Blue Ribbon while watching this fancy new contraption they call TV! Well, gollee!"*

What the fuck? The whole point of the show was that it's supposed to be a variety-talent show filmed in front of a LIVE audience. I was so naive and disappointed that I didn't know where to take it next, so the project was shelved. The very next year, I was stunned to see a show with a very similar format, variety acts featuring comics, singers, dancers, etc. It's a very successful show with celebrity judges and filmed in front of a LIVE audience. One of the producers of this program: Allen.

One fact I'm not sure if I've mentioned (maybe I have, but I've been writing for months and haven't edited yet), is that I haven't missed a Sunday of church since October, 2010. Actually (don't strike me down, Lord), I did miss one Sunday, but I made it up by going twice the following week. In October of 2010, Katie and I had the biggest fight of our relationship. I was being a selfish, insensitive prick. Although I was being the best father I could be, I was distant from Katie, and disrespectful. The thought of losing her and my two angels was inconceivable, so I decided to be a better man, and husband. Our family became regulars at St. Mel Catholic Church in Woodland Hills, and even though I'm not Catholic, I enjoy our weekly routine. Someone told me that you can tell your child to do something, but they learn by watching you. I wanted to lead by example.

By the way, if you're doing the math, this was before the cancer. I told Katie that I believe she had a Voodoo doll of me and stuck pins in the junk area. I'm a much better man and husband than I've ever been, but keep getting knocked down in my professional life. Before we had kids and I faced rejection, which is pretty much daily in this town, I would just pick myself up and hit the comedy stage and *bam!*-- problem solved! Many famous comics who have successful acting careers, but have continued to work as a stand-up will tell you that it's because no one can take that away from you. I made a decision to attempt to be a producer so I can spend more time with my family, but I keep getting knocked on my ass, just when things seem so fucking close. I admitted tonight to Katie, something that I have never admitted to anyone before, that there have been a couple of times when I've been lying awake at night, and have had dark thoughts. Would my family be better off without me? Are all of my efforts and hard work just hoop dreams?

Right after I receive the shitty news about my Rich Franklin show, our family sits down to dinner as we do every night. Colin sits right next to me, where we're usually joking around and having a great time. However, this night I am totally zoning out and wallowing in my misery over my bad news. I feel like everyone is speaking in that voice on *Charlie Brown*—"Wah wah wha wha," when Colin chimes in and says "Hey, Daddy,

I've got five new dance moves I want to show you." With that, he jumped up from the dinner table and started busting out his five awesome new dances and moves. Seeing my little pride and joy so excited totally made me snap out of my funk. I realized that this is what it's all about—when life knocks you on your ass, just say "fuck it," jump up and bust out five new dance moves! Hammer Time!

Dec 13
Kaiser Lab (and Scout)

Back again for my blood work that Dr. Ravari ordered. This will be my third PSA test since my surgery. Only a few hours after my visit, I begin to receive email notices that my lab results are coming in. I log onto the Kaiser site to start checking things out. I see lots of abbreviations but I have no idea what any of them mean. They only thing that matters to me are the numbers. Everything is broken done into three-letter abbreviations: CRE, ICU, IUD. I scan to the right and see a column with the range of the numbers. After several days of checking these numbers, I learn that I am within the healthy range of them all. The health is on track. It's "Dance Party USA" at the D house. Let's keep this party train rollin'!

27

Christmas

I was originally supposed to have my biopsy last December 24th, but I decided to wait until January. I didn't want to ruin our Christmas celebrations, in the event that the results were positive, which they turned out to be. In reflection of time since, I have so much to be thankful for— Katie, who is my best friend, our beautiful kiddos who fill my heart with joy every day, our family, friends and my health.

I have always loved Christmas, even when I was poor as a child. I think back and remember how my mom would put our gifts on lay-a-way starting in the summer. I also remember being a total brat one year and expressing my disappointment on not getting the G.I. Joe I had asked for. My mom had tried her best and got me a knock-off, generic action doll named Safari Sam, or something, and I was like, "What the F is this?" Although I'm sure I didn't say the "F" word or Mama would've hit me with a lamp. Sorry for not understanding the true meaning of Christmas, Mama. I wish I had that Safari Sam set right now. I bet Colin would love it.

I usually get annoyed at people living in L.A. this time of year, because everyone tries to be so fucking PC that's it's hard to get a "Merry Christmas" out of people for fear that they might offend someone who isn't Christian. Katie and I were hiking one year on Christmas day when we passed two ladies coming our way. I smiled and said, "Merry Christmas" and they just looked at me and kept on walking. I flipped a switch said, "What the fuck is wrong with people that can't even say 'Merry Christmas' back to me? Shit, you bitches made me lose my Christmas spirit!" I'm sure Jesus would understand this outburst.

Almost every house in my hometown back in Kentucky decorates for the holidays. Even in the poorest part of town you'll see lots of Christmas decorations. You might see a washer and dryer on out on the front porch, but they will have a string of Christmas lights on them. In L.A., it's like, "Hey, somebody in Woodland Hills has an inflatable Frosty the Snowman in their front yard! Get the kids, let's go check it out!" Woo-hoo!

This was the first Christmas I truly just wanted to give and see the joy on other peoples' faces. I've already gotten the most important gift I could ever wish for this year—my life.

Arrowhead- One Last Hoorah!

What a crazy year it has been. Looks like another chapter is about to be turned. Katie's parents have just finalized the deal on a new home in Oxnard, California, near Santa Barbara. They'll be moving in February and selling their home in Arrowhead that they bought shortly after Mr. Farrell's retirement. This move is bittersweet for me. I was looking forward to enjoying some summers on the lake with the kiddos. Lake Arrowhead is a mellow mountain resort town about an hour and a half outside of Los Angeles. If I would have spent my youth in a community like this, I would have totally terrorized this tranquil little hideaway.

We are going to be here for New Years' Eve, along with some of Katie's family. This New Years' day will also mark the 30th anniversary of my dad's death.

January 1, 2012

Well, here it is. I really didn't think I would be so reflective and sad, but Katie's sister, Erin, asked me about my dad and I almost started to cry. The irony of the situation has also hit me. Here I am, so full of memories of him and thinking how unfair it all is, and all the while I'm not sure of my own future. Will I even be around to see my own kids grow up? So many changes have taken place this year. I remember reading the book *The Alchemist* and about all the struggles and challenges the author faced. I don't know what God's plan is for me, but there isn't time to be bitter or feel sorry for myself about anything. Just keep getting back up and rockin'!

I always felt the need to be wanted. From my days as a lonely kid watching other kids play with their dads, I wanted that so badly that I think I overcompensated by striving for attention. I always thought once I was famous I would be truly happy and feel validated. Going through cancer has really made me realize that the only thing that matters in life is family. Period! I have tasted a little success, but the joy of that success doesn't even come close to the joy in my heart I get when one of my kiddos says, "Daddy, I love you." If I had gotten the cancer without Katie and her family in my life, I would be going through this ordeal all alone.

I wonder how things would be different if Dad were still alive. What would he teach my kids? How to make a trick pool shot, or ride a wheelie on a motorcycle? Even though my dad was tough, he was affectionate. He always told me he loved me until the day he died. I make Colin promise every day that we will always be best buddies, and not to forget it! He says, "I not forget it ever or next time!"

Last night (New Year's Eve) our two nieces and Colin were standing on the hearth of the fireplace, taking turns telling jokes and making up stories. The grown-ups kept pressuring me to tell a joke. People don't understand that comics don't tell jokes, unless you're a hundred years old and had formerly worked with Jack Benny. I finally got up there and told a story of a little boy who loved Hot Wheels so much that he had a special Hot Wheels book that he took to the potty (true story about Colin). His face red with humiliation, and without missing a beat, Colin stepped right up there and told a story about a little boy and his daddy. "I cannot tell his name," he said, and then went on to tell how the little boy's daddy would take him to Target and would not buy this little boy a Hot Wheels car. Touché!

Apparently, Colin was embarrassed that I would mention his private matters in public and thought of his rebuttal that quickly. As I was standing up there telling my story with Colin gazing up at me, it really hit home. I always want my children to admire me, not only as their father, but as a person. No high-speed cars chases with them, no absence ever, and always—not only telling them, but showing them how much I love them. *R.I.P. Dad. I bet you're holding court, wherever you are.*

The other night, after our nightly ritual of reading books, I showed a picture of my dad to Colin and explained that he was my daddy and his other grandfather. Colin said he wanted to meet him and I didn't know exactly what to say, with Colin being only 3. It is very rare that I am ever speechless. I said, "Well, he's in Heaven now." Colin just replied, "Well, I want to meet him, Daddy." Maybe someday you will, buddy.

January, 2012

We're off to a much better start this year! I signed a co-production agreement with the producers of Howie Mandel's show *Mobbed*.

I watched a very interesting documentary last night called *Fat, Sick and Almost Dead*. It showed a very over-weight man who is on many medications because of his poor health. He goes on a 60-day juice fast and it changes his life. In addition to losing a ton of weight, his energy level increases, he thinks more clearly, and all of his stats improve so much that he no longer needs medication. Our society depends too much on medications. People pollute their bodies with saturated fats, sugars, additives, pesticides, hormones, drugs and alcohol. As a result, their quality of life sucks. People order every piece of junk on late night infomercials looking for a quick fix to get healthy or lose weight. We have the only country in the world with fat poor people!

I chose to take care of my body a long time ago. I have exercised since the day I arrived in Los Angeles, and although I did abuse it with some alcohol consumption, for the most part, I'm the healthiest guy I know! For a period of time, I was so fanatical about eating only quality calories that I would measure my food to make sure I was getting the right amount of nutrients and calories. One friend whom I've known for over 20 years told me that when he found out about my cancer, he said to his wife, "I've got to get checked immediately! Stevie

D. is the healthiest motherfucker I know, so if he has one cell of cancer in his body, I have 100!"

There was a story on ABC's *Nightline* featuring Dr. David Agus. He is the doctor that my friend and producing partner, Arleen Sorkin, put me in touch with when I was diagnosed. The reporter on this story, Bill Weir, said Dr. Agus is the man you call when you are very rich and very sick. I am not very rich, but was very fortunate enough to have Arleen in my life when I was freaking out and needed some advice, immediately! Dr. Agus treated Lance Armstrong and Steve Jobs, so to say I was lucky that he would take time to give me any advice would be an understatement. When I was torn between Dr. Chuang and Dr. Williams, Arleen asked Dr. Agus a simple question, "If it were your son having the surgery, which doctor would you go with?" He said, "Dr. Williams." My decision was made—end of story. The *Nightline* piece was about a bestselling book that Dr. Agus had written titled *The End of Illness*. The book is apparently about the early detection of diseases through controversial techniques.

In a show of good sportsmanship, in the *Nightline* report, Bill Weir has a calcium scan and learns that he is at high risk for a heart attack within five years. He is in his mid-40s and works out regularly, but because of his high-stress job, he has a clogged artery. Oh, great, my stress level is on 11 every day! Some days, I make a Wall Street trader look like he's meditating! I now make it a point every day to do one very important thing—breathe. Even while sitting in L.A. traffic, which has been proven to be the most stressful in the nation, I try to relax, reflect, and just breathe. This usually works, unless of course, Ryan Seacrest is on the radio, and then all bets are off.

28

The Offspring-

Katie and I decided not to find out what the sex of our baby was going to be. This can be exciting, but also nerve racking when you're preparing. If I had known we were having a boy, I would've painted his room some manly color, like black, and put some art on the walls. And by art, I mean posters of hot rods and motorcycles. But we decided to torture our friends and family and not find out.

Katie had a brutal delivery lasting 22 hours! We had a cool room at Cedars-Sinai Hospital in Beverly Hills, but unfortunately for Katie, she wasn't able to enjoy it. She had a dangerously high fever and because of the position of the baby, she was placed on her side facing the wall, so she wasn't able to enjoy our beautiful view. At one point it seemed like they were about to do an emergency C-section because the baby's heart rate was slowing down, but our uber nurse sprung into action and immediately rolled Katie onto her back, placed her hands on Katie's stomach and began to violently shake her. I was about to karate-chop this woman, when we noticed the baby's heart rate on the monitor going back up to normal. Whew! She then casually informed us that the baby didn't like that other position. *Really? Couldn't the baby have just knocked three times on Katie's stomach and let us know?* Katie was miserable, shivering uncontrollably, even though it was the middle of July and she was covered up to her neck in blankets. Somewhere around the 18th hour, our doctor came in and said, "It's go time!"

Ok, let's do it! Where do I wash up? I imagined we were about to be directed to some high-tech operating room, with giant robot-looking machines and a large staff of nurses. Where are my scrubs? Our doctor introduced us to another nurse and said, "You're standing in the operating room!" He then asked me, "Now, at which end do you want to be standing?" I had promised Katie that I would not be looking down there in her business, but I didn't want to be at the other end in the cheap seats, either. I told the doctor I wanted to help. "Ok," she said, "Then you take the left leg and the nurse will take the right."

Alright, let's rock! How long could this possibly take? Twenty minutes, at the most? Damn, I should've brought my notepad; I could've gotten some good material out of this. Ninety minutes later, the doctor is now getting frustrated and concerned, and so are we. She believes that Katie isn't pushing hard enough, so she does a sneaky trick and shuts off her epidural. Ouch!

I push Katie's leg up in rhythm with the doctor's counts, but still no baby! Finally the doctor sees the head, but it seems to be stuck! After another hour or so, the doctor announces that the baby is finally coming out! I take a deep breath before I turn to see what it is. I always thought I would be able to handle a girl better, since I grew up in a household with them. Just as I turn, I hear the doctor saying, "Come on little guy—breathe!" Colin was born with his umbilical cord wrapped around his neck, and because of the difficult delivery, the little guy was really struggling to live. It's the most helpless feeling in the world when your child is in trouble and there is nothing you can do to help.

The doctor finally gets my little man to breathe, and a crack team rushes in to start performing tests on him. They whisk him over to a table and ask if I'd like to cut the cord . Of course I would. Although I would've preferred to use my personal buck knife, which would've made for a much cooler story, apparently there are some sorts of hygiene rules at these fancy city hospitals, so they hand me a pair of sterilized scissors to do the trick. By the way, the umbilical cord is surprisingly rubbery and took several attempts. Katie only got to hold the little man for a few minutes before they took him away. His face was swollen and purple because of the rough time he had coming into this world. The nurses actually put a sign on his bassinet that read, "Dupin baby has purple face. Please do not try to resuscitate."

It's amazing that a hospital will just hand over a baby to the parents and send you on your way without even an owner's manual. As we put Colin in the car to head home, I kept suspiciously looking at the nurse, expecting her to say, "Ha, ha, just joking, you hillbilly. Give me that baby back!" As I drive home 20 miles per hour under the speed limit, the reality hits me—*This little angel is your responsibility. DO NOT FUCK THIS UP!* After spending a couple of days with the little guy, I had to get back to work. It tore my heart out to leave my little man. As I rode my motorcycle over the hills from the Valley back to Hollywood, tears rolled down my cheeks. There have only been a few days since that we've been apart.

Hollywood is not the town to slack off, if you want to make it. You bust your ass, making many sacrifices to get your break. Things were starting to happen for me. The plan was that when the *Rockstars of Comedy* DVD was released, I was going to kick the career into overdrive—tour, television appearances, hotels, parties, and money, money, money! But all of that changed when Colin came into my life. I couldn't imagine leaving this little man to go out on tour and promote right now. I did not want leave this little guy now or ever! Damn, am I finally growing up? This is scary!

I can't imagine a dad and son being closer than Colin and me. I'm sure a lot of dads say that, but when he was born, I felt a love I didn't even know I was capable of feeling. He used to cry every night around 2:00 a.m. so I would rock him and sing him back to sleep. One of the songs I would sing is *You Are My Sunshine*, and every time I sang it, I would get teary-eyed, and I still do. We are so close that one morning, I woke up and told Katie that I had a dream that Colin had pooped in his sleep. Katie just laughed because Colin had never pooped in his sleep before. I went in his room and smelled that unforgettable stench, and sure enough, he had pooped. I am the Poop Whisperer!

You Gotta Have Faith

Faith was born 23 months after Colin. Here I am again, with Katie at the hospital and with the same fears, doubts and excitement as I had the first time around. Faith's delivery was much easier than my little guy. It was almost like going through a drive-thru: "Would you like to super-size that?"

"No, we'll just take a normal-sized baby, please!"

Faith is my little dreamboat. These damn kids are so cute, it's hard for me to get any work done, because I don't want to miss a second with them. Every night after dinner, we usually have dance party which sometimes includes Faith tearing her diaper off and doing what she calls the "Bum Bum Dance." Please don't alert child services— it's just the way the D Family parties. Usually the kiddos hit the sack around 8:30ish and we are right behind them. These kids have me wrapped around their fingers, and that's just where I want to be.

Colin and Faith couldn't be more different. They both have a deep sweetness. However, Faith is more like an M&M— hard on the outside, soft on the inside. She is the ringleader and, as she reminds us, the "bosh" (boss). Colin is my sidekick, and as I've said since the day he was born, my main man. A few months ago we were at a family event, and for the first time he was completely independent, wrestling and playing with his cousins all day. It was a bittersweet feeling as I watched him— my little man is growing up. When I tucked him that I night, I said to him, "Hey, buddy, I watched you playing with your cousins today. You're getting to be such a big boy. Daddy is very proud of you."

I guess I expected him just to say a sleepy "thank you" or "good night" and that would be it. However, to my surprise, he looked at me with sadness in his eyes and said, "But, Daddy, I still need you to be close to me." As the Rolling Stones sang, "Wild horses couldn't drag me away." I will always be right here.

I thank God for Katie everyday. She is the best mother I could've ever asked for our children. She's the one that keeps this crazy train on track around here and keeps our kiddos from being complete heathens. When it's just me with them, its party time! Katie has come home on a few occasions when they're on my watch and asked, "What did the kids have for dinner?" to which I reply, "Dinner? Oops, guess we got a little carried away playing WrestleMania and Dance Party."

I've decided that, instead of trying to recap some of the highlights of great times we've had, or funny shit they've said, I'll let a few recent Facebook status updates do that for me...

November 13, 2013

Conversation with my 4-year-old and 2-year-old in my car:
Colin: Daddy, I like this song.
Me: Yes, buddy, it's Bob Seger.
Faith: I don't like Bob Seger. Is he a bad guy?
Colin: No, he's a rock star!
Faith: I like Bob Seger.

November 1, 2012

Taking Colin to school with eyeliner still on. It's only rock n' roll but I like it!

October 2012

My 2-year-old daughter just told me she gave big, mean boys in the bouncy house knuckle sandwiches last night. That's my girl! Santa may put mini-brass knuckles in her stocking this year!

November 2012

When will I learn that I can't party like I used to? Two hours in the bouncy house is too much!

November 2012

Following our dinner prayer, I ask Colin what he is thankful for. His answer: "I'm thankful for all the people in the world, even the ones that died and dogs that have died." I ask Faith what she is thankful for. Her answer: "Mmm, Hello Kitty."

November 2012

Just told Colin he can be anything he wants to be when he grows up. So I say, what do you want to be? He says, "A Muppet!"

And that pretty much some sums it up. Give your children love and freedom to express themselves, and encourage them to be anything they dream they can be. Even if it's a Muppet.

Colin and Faith, you are my sunshine.

29

Chew Toy

Week of March 12, 2012

I opened a letter a couple of days ago from the office of Dr. Williams. Could he have discovered something? Did he learn that Kaiser had made a terrible mistake and he removed the prostate of the wrong patient? No, this is a reminder of my one-year follow-up appointment on March 15th.

Oh, yeah, now I remember—that little procedure that changed my life last St. Paddy's Day. I am also reminded that I have to do another PSA test before the appointment that is in four days. Nothing like waiting until the last minute! I stop by the Woodland Hills Kaiser and get my blood test done. It's becoming routine. Everything is all about efficiency for me. Even when I'm shopping in the grocery store: I always grab two or three baskets instead of pushing a cart. I dash up and down the aisles like I'm running with the bulls in Spain, jumping over displays and knocking down old ladies. "Lookout, Grandma, got to hit the produce and get out of here!" They say time is money, but I say time is time—I don't know how much I have, so I hustle!

Tuesday, March 13, 2012

The PSA test comes back at .01 again. I still have no idea why it would read any number at all, but I make a mental note to ask Dr. Williams to refresh my memory about this on Thursday.

I am looking forward to seeing Dr. Williams, but I have a bittersweet feeling, like I'm losing my security blanket. Our next appointment isn't for another six months after this one, so I'm really going to torture him with questions, and more questions. I don't know if a physical exam will be involved, but if it is, he may find a surprise—yesterday, a dog bit my junk. That's right, you read correctly. I was at Bob and Cindy Broder's house, wrestling her 95-pound Golden Retriever, when he bit down on my penis! *Hey, Lassie, that's not an effin' chew toy!* The good news is the nerves are definitely working, because it hurt like hell! Now why doesn't this happen more often? Or *does* it, and people just don't speak of it? Now what do you do when a dog bites your penis? Do you tell the owner, and if so, how? "Hey, your dog just bit down on my junk like a chew toy."

The scene of Ben Stiller's penis getting stuck in his zipper in *There's Something About Mary* comes to mind. I imagine the neighbors rushing over, everyone examining the wound, saying, "Hey, let's put some antiseptic on there! How about a Mickey Mouse band-aid?" I silently scream and decide not to tell Cindy, who is only a few feet away, with her back turned to me.

As soon as I get into my car, I unzip my pants to examine my wound. The Broders just happen to live a few doors down from Justin Timberlake in the Hollywood Hills. I usually park closer to Justin's house because it's much easier to turn around, when I leave. Justin has a guard and security cameras in front of his property. I imagine the police suddenly pulling up to arrest me for indecent exposure. I can see the headlines of *The Hollywood Reporter* : "Comedian Stevie D. Arrested in Front of Justin Timberlake's House with Penis in Hand!" I should only be so lucky to make the headlines of *The Hollywood Reporter*.

The wounds aren't that bad, but I definitely have distinctive teeth marks on my penis. Maybe when Dr. Williams asks about sexual activity, I can drop my underwear say, "You see these teeth marks on my penis don't you, Doc? You can use this example for your lectures." And then he high fives me as we laugh.

March 15th

I arrive in lovely Riverside, California at 9:29 a.m., after a two-hour drive. My appointment is scheduled for 9:30. You would think I would be stressed about such a close call, but it's funny how things like this don't seem to bother me too much these days. I sit waiting for Dr. Williams for 45 minutes, but it's still all good! *Ohmmm.*

The man with the golden hands finally strides in, exuding confidence and empathy, as usual. After exchanging pleasantries, we get down to business. I pull out my Blackberry for a list of questions, from myself and Katie. Number one, and the most important on this list, is "Why do I still have to do a PSA when I no longer have a prostate?" I imagine he's thinking, "Haven't we been over this?" *Yes, we have, and we'll probably go over it again, when I see you in six months.* He again explains it to me.

Dr. Williams then asks how the plumbing is functioning. He actually uses medical terms, but those are boring. I tell him that I don't have a problem with the incontinency, but I have a question about my erections. Now, when I get aroused, I have a curve in my penis. Not that I was planning on doing *Playgirl*, but I'm concerned. He tells me that this is not uncommon; it is probably caused by the amount of scar tissue. He asks how often Katie and I are romantic. I tell him not often enough, with our crazy schedules and the kiddos. I'm starting to be alarmed. In the beginning of my recovery, a vacuum pump device is recommended. This device looks like something that you would order from the Adam and Eve erotic products catalog that would come in a plain brown wrapper. Since I was getting erections without using these kinky devices, I discussed this with Dr. Williams early on, and he suggested that I didn't need it. I never asked how many I should be getting a day. Now I'm paranoid. Am I not getting enough? I need lots of blood flow to be happening in my junk area! I ask if he will write me a doctor's note for those massages with "happy endings." He laughs.

I am relieved that he doesn't expect me to get erect so he can examine me. "Hey, Steve, we have a collection of porn here. What are you into—girl on girl? Fetish? Oh , that's right, you're from Kentucky—how about something involving small farm animals? I'm going to step out of the room for a few minutes, enjoy!" Luckily, he doesn't need to see the curve and goes on to explain that because of the severity of the surgery, especially removing the lymph nodes, this will more than likely correct itself. I take the opportunity to tell him about the dog bite. He finds this story humorous and takes my word for it. Thanks for sparing me any further humiliation, Dr. Williams.

I am happy to report that the curve has since corrected itself. I'm once again a straight shooter, except that I'm shooting blanks. I've been contemplating how much detail I will go into on this subject, but if I'm going to be honest about my life, then I'll have to let it all hang out... so to speak. OK, here we go...

One of the men I had spoken to before my surgery was a friend of a friend, who was gay and 72 (once again, average age of prostate cancer patients). This man, Irving, is quite a character, usually sharing way more information than a person needs to know. I was more than ready to get off the phone with Irving when he said something that freaked me out. He said that when he orgasms, nothing comes out. He then went into graphic detail about acts he would perform on his lovers. I really didn't need any visuals of his sexploits, but this information was nonetheless alarming. I pretended not to be too shaken, because I didn't want Irving to share any more details of his adventures with his boy toys. After we hung up, I convinced myself that this fact must be chalked up to Irving's age. He was probably ejaculating dirt before the surgery. I ask Dr. Williams about this and, unfortunately, he concurred with the perverted grandpa. The prostate is responsible for producing sperm, as well as controlling urine flow, so although I would still be able to have orgasms, they would be internal. I can't explain the medical mechanics, but everything works, only with less mess! Now I understand a little better what Sting was talking about when he bragged of Tantric sex skills. Hey, maybe I should do a public service announcement? *"Prostatectomy has its benefits. If Bill Clinton would've had one, Monica wouldn't have paraded the DNA dress around like it was the first flag sewn by Betsy Ross."*

30

The Judge's Daughter

I met my wife Katie through a mutual friend, Connie, whom she worked with at an art gallery in Beverly Hills. Connie was an aspiring actress-model type, referred to in L.A. as a MAW (model, actress, whatever). Connie and I met at a nightclub in Century City shortly after I arrived in Los Angeles. This particular club was known for being very difficult to gain access to, unless you were a recognizable face, pretty girl, or rich dude. The doorman, Mark, had come from Studio 54 in New York, so getting past him was no easy feat. These types of doormen have no soul. They have the power to crush a group of partygoers' spirits in 10 seconds.

Group of guys to doorman: "Hi, I'm here with three of my buddies.It's my birthday and we're here to celebrate!"

Doorman: "Well, you might want to try Chuck E. Cheese, because you're not coming in here."

However, this Hollywood hillbilly could not be deterred by this humorless clown. I noticed right away a man in a black suit who would come out every so often to survey the crowd waiting behind the velvet rope. *This* is the man holding the keys to the castle, because he was the promoter. He immediately became my BFF (best friends forever). I got his attention and used my gift of gab to win him over. Within minutes he instructed Mark to let my friends and me in. I would come in weekly with my crew, and as Mark reluctantly unhooked the rope, I would blow him an air kiss as we breezed by. Upon entering we did see a lot of pretty people, but most of the attractive girls would be sitting with older men. I was so naïve at the time, I really didn't get it. How could these old farts be any fun? I later caught on—the rich men finance these girls' lifestyles.

I did have one secret weapon that that the geezers didn't have— I could bust a move. And that's how I got the attention of Connie, who also loved to dance. Connie and I have remained friends ever since.

One late summer Friday night in 2000, Connie invited Katie to come with her to see me perform at the Comedy Store in Hollywood. The story goes that when Katie arrived at Connie's place to pick her up, Connie took one look at her (out of her conservative work uniform) and said, "My friend is going to fall in love with you!" She should've worked for the Psychic Friends Network, because that's exactly what happened. I was more of the "fall in lust" type, but the very first sight of Katie was a game changer. As I approached the club, I immediately spotted Connie and the future Mrs. D. Besides being tall and stunning, she had an air of coolness and an attitude that told me she did not want to be at a comedy club on a Friday night. I love a challenge, and I could tell immediately, this was going to be a monumental one. I thought, "I've really got to do something to impress this girl immediately. First impression is everything." When I'm nervous, my defense mechanism usually tells me to try to be funny, so I ran up and bit Connie on the ass! Classy guy, huh? I don't think Katie was too impressed, but luckily she didn't turn and leave.

Now on this particular night I was wearing my usual type of attire— a purple Prince t-shirt (with the sleeves cut out, of course), and leather pants. I escorted the two ladies in and gave them a choice seat on the aisle so I could have access to flirt with Katie throughout the show. I had a good set that night, so I was feeling extra cocky and began to turn on the charm, or B.S. (it's in the eye of the beholder). I remember Katie asked me what else I did, and I told her I was a porn star. I also asked her to be the queen of my double wide. Smooth talker!

Now, get your pen and paper fellas, because here's a tip straight out the *Player's Handbook*: Women are very competitive. If a guy can manage to date a hot girl, chances are that other girls are going to wonder why in the hell she is dating him, and then they'll try to steal him. There would be no other girl who who could compete with Katie, but on this night I had invited another girl to my show—a fitness model I had met at the gym. The "other" girl in question had consumed enough cocktails to encourage her to shout my name loudly throughout this evening (even while other comics where on stage). I have been reminded of this many times over the years, so I know she left an impression. Now just to make sure my bets are covered, I invited Connie and Katie to a dance club, as well as the fitness model and her friends. Don't hate the player!

I knew for sure that Katie was different from other girls I had dated, because when we were at the club, she asked if I was close to my family. I gave her the best answer I could think of: "Uh, well actually, they're over 2,000 miles away, but they're in my heart. Now can we bust a move?" She told me she and her family were very close. I thought , *"Uh, oh, this isn't some jaded former homecoming queen like L.A.is so full of. I'm really going have to play my cards right here."*

Katie wasn't kidding. She is from a very close Irish Catholic family. She grew up in the San Fernando Valley, along with her four siblings—two brothers and two sisters. Oh, and by the way, did I mention that her father is 6'6," 300 pounds, and a judge? However, it was months before I got the opportunity to meet her parents. I imagined our meeting would go something like this: I pull up to her parents' home in my 79' Trans Am—with T-top off, of course—park right on the lawn, and jump out without opening my door, NASCAR-style. I take her father a six-pack of Budweiser as a good will gesture, and then apologize for drinking a few on the way over. Her parents are conservative Republicans and begin to question me on my political views. I tell them that I don't register to vote because I believe I may still have warrants in Kentucky. I explain that although I may not know all of the GOP candidates, I can name all of the characters on *The Dukes of Hazzard*. "Now who wants a Bud?" I imagine that it would be around this time that Katie's father grabs his phone to call the local authorities for a background check on me, as I jump into my car and peel the Kentucky Porshe out of the yard!

Actually, Katie's father and I hit it off very well. I met her parents for the first time at her grandmother's wake. I was hesitant about going, expecting a very sad ceremony. But when I arrived there was an Irish band playing, with friends and relatives drinking, dancing and having a great time. Damn, I want to have an Irish wake when I go! Katie greeted me and led me to her father for our introduction. As I followed her through the living room, I saw this huge, imposing man walking toward me. I tried to remain calm, but I was actually thinking, "This could be it for me." This giant of man has just lost his mother, and now his daughter, whom who he sent to nice, private Catholic schools, is bringing this white-trash, hillbilly into his home? I really thought Mr. Farrell was going to go off me! I don't think people even use that term anymore, but that's what he was going to do. Instead, it went something like this:

Katie: "Dad, this is Steve, the guy I was telling you about."

Me: "Hi, Mr. Farrell, or should I call you, Your Honor? It's a pleasure to meet you, sir. I'm very sorry about your mother."

Mr. Farrell: "It's Mike, and thank you. Now go get a beer!"

And we've gotten along great ever since. Mr. Farrell is a self-made man. I believe he respects the fact that I'm a hard-working, straight-shooting S.O.B. who takes care of his family. The Irish and the hillbillies have also faced similar adversities. Besides bluegrass and Irish music sounding very similar, the Irish also have their own version of moonshine called poitín. Hell, maybe we're not that different after all. They now have an outlaw for an in-law.

I was on my best behavior as I slowly started easing my way into this respectable family. One of the first holiday celebrations at her parents' home was Easter. Up until this point, I don't believe her parents knew about my Trans Am, so I planned to keep it that way, at least until I could win them over a little more. My car was pretty much equivalent to a van with a bumpersticker that read, "If you see it rockin', don't bother knockin'!" I strategically parked the Kentucky Porshe a few houses away and walked to the Farrells', sporting a tie and carrying flowers: the perfect Southern gentleman. Katie's family has had the same protocol for their Easter festivities for decades. Unfortunately, I didn't get the memo. The "kids" (adult children) were ordered to go Katie's old bedroom in the back of the house, until the Easter Bunny came (seriously). As I sat in the room with Katie's siblings reading their childhood Easter books, her brother Mike walked into the room and asked, "Hey, Steve, is that your Trans Am parked up the street?" As all heads turned to me, I answered, "Yes, why?"

"Oh, you have a flat tire. Hey, let's read *'Here comes Peter Cottontail'*!"

To Katie's credit, instead of apologizing to her family for dating a hillbilly and lowering the family stock, she followed me outside to assist me in fixing my flat tire. By the time, we walked back into the house, sleeves rolled up, and hands greasy, it was announced, "The Easter Bunny has come!" Katie and her siblings barreled out the back door like brides-to-be at a wedding dress close-out sale! I didn't want to seem overzealous, so I slowly brought up the rear.

Had I known what a fierce competition this was, I would've stepped up my game. We each were given an empty plastic grocery bag as we stepped into the combat zone, a.k.a. the backyard. I was the last to enter and found Katie and her siblings running around like lunatics. The Easter Bunny had hidden eggs filled with delicious, chocolate treats around the yard. Or at least they looked delicious, judging by the siblings who were scoring already. I was zig-zagging around the yard, but every time I got close to a hotspot, another sibling would've just beat me. After about five minutes, the brothers and sisters had pretty much swept all the areas of the yard, and began retreating to the porch with their treats.

At this point, I started to really pick up my pace and began frantically scouring the premises, with no luck, to the family's amusement. The harder I looked, the harder they laughed. I looked like a dragster trying to break the land speed record with my empty plastic bag flying in the air like a parachute behind me. All of the participants had stopped searching, except for me, as her mother announced, "There's one egg left, and no one gets their Easter basket until Steve finds it!" This is torture! I was now sweating profusely and determined to find that damned egg. As the family laughed and ridiculed me, they began to coach me like a five-year-old: "You're getting warmer,

warmer…oops! Cold, colder." In my state of humiliation I didn't even pick up that every time I got close to their father, who was sitting on the patio, they would announce, "Getting hot!" Finally, they must've thought this game would go on for days because her mother told me where the egg was hidden, under Mr. Farrell's chair. What? That's not fair! It never even crossed my mind to go searching under there. I can only imagine her father's reaction, "Steve, what in the hell are you doing? I think you've seen *Deliverance* too many times!" At this time, her father picked up the egg and taunted me with it. In a gesture of pity, I was still given an Easter basket. It's "survival of the fittest" in the Farrell family. I was determined to redeem myself the next Easter. Even if that meant covert operations, satellite images, blueprints of the property—whatever it takes.

Unfortunately, the following Easter was a repeat performance of the fumbling hillbilly. As we were shoving our way out the backdoor, I knocked Katie's sister, Colleen, to the ground. I had spotted an egg in a tree outside, and in my excitement, leveled her. "Should I help her up? What if someone gets my egg? I only need one!" Hastily, I pulled Colleen to her feet as she sprung out the door, ran and snatched my egg! I was 0 for 2 at this bloodthirsty Easter egg game! Luckily, Katie's parents moved to Lake Arrowhead later that year, and the tradition was over for the grown-up kids. (That story was for my friend, Mitch Mullany, who after hearing it, laughed his ass off, saying it was the most pathetic thing he'd ever heard. I hope you're getting some laughs retelling it in Heaven. R.I.P., buddy.)

Katie's mother Susan (who BTW, didn't acknowledge me for the first several months of our courtship, and I don't blame her), taught her girls an extremely valuable lesson: never show a man your cards. Always keep him guessing and pursuing. Katie had this lesson down to a tee! Alright, ladies, take note here—if you are on your thihrd date and you start talking about marriage, even though the man may act like he's down for that plan, he's really thinking, "This chick is fucking bonkers" and he will probably run for the hills. Now with that being said, here's another chapter out of the *Players Handbook*: If a man has been dating a girl for six months and she hasn't mentioned marriage or a future, he will. Of course, he doesn't mean it; he is just feeling the situation out, and testing you to make sure he has you on lockdown.

After about a year, Katie hadn't mentioned anything of this sort. Actually, we has been dating four months before I finally asked her, "Are you my girlfriend?"

She casually replied, "Yes." So, after about a year of dating, I had to implement a player's mind game on her, but Katie didn't take the bait. I would say things like, "I see us sharing a home in the hills someday... doesn't that sound nice?"

She would usually respond with something like, "Well, I don't know who I'm going to marry."

Marry? Who said anything marriage? And what do you mean, you don't know who you are going to marry? She was supposed to say something like, "That sounds like a dream come true." Damn, this girl is good!

Cut to three years later, and I'm standing at the altar as Katie walks toward me looking absolutely breathtaking, and I am thinking to myself, "Ah, ha, *now* do you know who you're going to marry? I guess I showed you, woman!" And then I realize that she executed a perfect Jedi mind trick on me, and thank God she did! Who knows where I would be if Katie hadn't taken me and inspired me to clean up my act? Hell, I even wear shirts with sleeves now. Occasionally.

I plan to instill those same values in our daughter. While Katie gives Faith's future boyfriend the cold shoulder, I'll be in the back yard hiding the Easter eggs where he could never find them.

Katie, you are my best friend, and the best thing that could've ever happened to me. Thank you for believing in us. Ladies, my message to you is this: Make the man work! If he isn't willing to work, he doesn't deserve you. Now, Katie, where's my damn beer? *Kidding.*

31

Dream On

I was planning on ending this book at my one-year anniversary, hopefully with a clean bill of health, and at least one of my television projects sold to a major network. I imagined that I would ride off into the sunset, but instead of a black stallion, I would be kicking up dust in my *Smokey and the Bandit* edition Trans Am. However, I've learned you can't live your life waiting for something to happen. Besides the cancer, this past year has been only a very small example of the struggles I've faced in my career. The rejections I face are actually much harder on Katie. Inside of my wedding ring, she inscribed, "I believe in you." I am so grateful this woman has had my back throughout my many battles. Now I know what Rocky meant when he said, "Yo Adrienne!" There have also been other developments that have caused me to take closer look at what's really the most important things in life.

First and foremost, I recently went in for my blood work that I now have to do every six months for the next five years. The very good news is that, once again, my PSA is .01. All good in the hood, or shall I say, under the hood. Although, I'm excited about the results, I've been told by someone very familiar with prostate and other forms of cancer that I should also do C-scan? Apparently this procedure detects hot or heated areas in your body that could be cancer. Oy! (Yiddish for either "fucking great" or "something else to worry about"). I'm also supposed to go back to the dreadful Riverside Kaiser and see the Man with the Golden Hands, Dr. Williams. Note to self, ask about this scan.

In the meantime, my surreal life in Hollywood continues. This is the city where one day you could be a barista slinging lattes in Starbucks, and the next day you're on a sitcom.

Just yesterday I was on a conference call with Maury Povich discussing one of my projects that he's interested in. As we were talking, I kept waiting for him to shout, "Stevie D., you are NOT the father," at which time I would've broken out into the Running Man Dance.

In another twist of fate, Katie's oldest sister, Erin, has been diagnosed with breast cancer and is currently undergoing three months of chemo before her double mastectomy surgery. Erin is a tough lady and proud mother of three who is handling things with grace and humor. Just the other day, she texted a pic of herself wearing the mane of the lion from *The Wizard of Oz*, with the caption, "How do you like my new wig?" Now that's courage.

The term "hero" seems to be everywhere these days. With the economy doing so poorly, I believe the media throws in this buzz word to attempt to lift people's spirits. Hell, I even used it to for one of my projects, *Hot Rod Heroes*. The actual definition of "hero" or "heroine" is "a character who, in the face of danger and adversity or from a position of weakness, displays courage nd the will for self-sacrifice—that is, heroism—for some greater good of all humanity."

There is also something in the Bible about worshipping false idols, but apparently I didn't pay enough attention at my Southern Baptist Church as a child to have it memorized. Lance Armstrong has probably raised more money for cancer than any other athlete in history. Although he is a cancer survivor himself, and an incredible athlete, I have never had the urge to run down to my local bike store and spend $5000 on a bike and deck myself out in U.S. Postal Service spandex. By the way, Lance got paid millions to represent the Postal Service and he got his bikes for free. It's called sponsorship. However, Lance was recently stripped of all of his Tour de France titles for refusing to testify in the investigatin into his alleged steroid use. If I were still doing stand-up, here's where I would say, "I bet he would give his left nut to get those titles back," but of course I'm more evolved now. *Wink.*

In any case, does doing steroids mean that Lance is no longer a hero? I would assume that to compete at that level, a lot of athletes are doing them. I didn't hear about the Union Cycliste Internationale or the United States Anti-Doping Agency going after the dude who came in last place. Lance has since admitting to doping, but what matters to me is the awareness his foundation has brought to cancer.

I recently found out what a true hero is one day when I received a request on Facebook. It was from a high school acquaintance who asked if I would take a "thumbs up" picture and post it on a page that was created in support of a little boy who was losing his battle with cancer. I immediately clicked the link to the little guy's page and was blown away by the number of supporters he and his family had. The boy's name was Lane Goodwin, and he just happened to be from my mom's hometown of Calhoun, Kentucky.

In March, 2010, Lane was diagnosed with stage IVAlveolar Rhabdomyosarcoma. He relapsed in July, 2011 and again in May, 2012. When the type of cancer has a name that is that difficult to pronounce, you know it's bad. The doctors at the Vanderbilt clinic had done all they could for Lane, but now had sent him home with only days—or perhaps hours—left to live. What started out with friends and members of this small community became a viral. Hundreds of thousands of people were touched by this brave little man's story as they sent him encouraging comments, along with "thumbs up" pictures.

His mother would frequently post updates and pictures of Lane. Throughout his battle, he remained all smiles. His mother would ask him if he was afraid to die, and he would say things like, "No, Mom, I got this." Where did this kid get so much courage? I followed Lane's story very closely during those weeks that he hung on, frequently checking updates, looking at the pictures of him smiling and always giving a thumbs up. I felt a sense of urgency, but helplessness at the same time. I got a few Hollywood friends to send thumbs up pics, and even tried to get recipes for green juices to boost his immune system sent to his mom. I remembered the feelings that I experienced when I was given the news that I had cancer. Suddenly I didn't care about my career, my image or my ego. All I could think about was my family. I could not imagine the feeling Lane's family must have felt, knowing that their precious angel would be leaving them.

I'm not sure if his story hit me more because he was from my hometown, or because I was a father now who had also had cancer, but like the thousands of others I prayed for a miracle. On October 17, 2012, little Lane Goodwin was free of suffering, as he finally lost his battle.

I spent a lot of time alone as a child, dreaming of escaping to some Nirvana, and to me that Nirvana was Hollywood. I was sure that once I was famous, I would be fulfilled, accepted, and loved. The story of this little guy from Kentucky reminded me that life is about the journey. Enjoy every day, because there is no guarantee of tomorrow (Insert *The Lion King*'s *Circle of Life*).

As I write this, I'm sitting in the very same Coffee Bean & Tea Leaf that I was in the morning after my diagnosis. I remember vividly speaking to Katie on my cell and stepping out of line as she told me all of the horrible things that could be in store for me. All I could think about was how I would give anything to have my health back. I was whining and feeling sorry for myself, and then a story comes along of a child who is given a death sentence and finds the inner strength to continue to shine.

Recently, I got the opportunity to step in front of the camera again. I was invited to be the guest on a web series called *Motivational Chat*. I had known the host, Jaimie Kalman, since she was a waitress in Miyagi's, a club on the Sunset Strip where I used to do a weekly comedy show. She now is a successful life coach in Beverly Hills. Jaime seemed to think that my story was inspirational and invited me to come on her show and share it. At first I thought, "Why would I go on a show where the guests are usually motivational speakers and self-help gurus?" However, after doing the show, something clicked and I thought, *Maybe this is what my purpose is— to inspire others.* Now that I think about it, the jobs that I've had are ones that make people feel good—deejay, fitness trainer and stand-up comic. It seems we don't always choose our paths; sometimes they choose us. If people happen to be inspired by my story, I am touched and humbled.I would never ask anyone to drink Kool Aid, but I will be happy to pass the moonshine jug. As AC/DC would say, "Have a drink on me."

"It's the possibility of having a dream come true that makes life interesting."

—Paulo Coelho

My loves.